Thomas Osborne Davis, Thomas Wallis

National and Historical Ballads, Songs and Poems

Thomas Osborne Davis, Thomas Wallis

National and Historical Ballads, Songs and Poems

ISBN/EAN: 9783744795265

Printed in Europe, USA, Canada, Australia, Japan

Cover: Foto ©Thomas Meinert / pixelio.de

More available books at **www.hansebooks.com**

NATIONAL

AND

HISTORICAL BALLADS,

SONGS, AND POEMS.

BY THOMAS DAVIS, M.R.I.A.

A NEW AND REVISED EDITION.

The sun set; but set not his hope:
Stars rose; his faith was earlier up:
Fixed on the enormous galaxy,
Deeper and older seemed his eye:
And matched his sufferance sublime
The taciturnity of time.
He spoke, and words more soft than rain
Brought the Age of Gold again:
His action won such reverence sweet,
As hid all measure of the feat.

Emerson.

DUBLIN:
JAMES DUFFY, 15, WELLINGTON-QUAY.
LONDON: 22, PATERNOSTER-ROW.
1869.

DUBLIN)
Printed by J. M. O'Toole & Son,
6 AND 7, GT. BRUNSWICK-ST.

CONTENTS.

PART V.—MISCELLANEOUS POEMS.

ADVERTISEMENT.

I HAVE spared no pains to make this volume as correct and complete as a first edition can be expected to be. But there were obstacles in the way, which no solicitude on my part could overcome. The reader will bear in mind, that one half of these poems were never collected during the author's lifetime, and that many of them had never received the slightest revision since their first appearance in the columns of a weekly journal. Thrown off, too, during the brief intervals of leisure, which his multifarious pursuits afforded, they could seldom have obtained that complete finish which would have precluded the necessity of their revision.

The classification and order under which they appear is altogether the work of the Editor. It has been his aim to group them in such a manner as by contrast or sequency, to make them throw light upon each other, and produce their full effect. The passages from MR. DAVIS's prose writings have been inserted with the same view.

A partial attempt has been made in a few of the ballads, to restore the Irish names of places and persons to their correct forms. But from the opposite character of the two languages, many difficulties arose, and the alterations have been confined to a few of the Ballads in Part III. MR. DAVIS was a warm advocate of the restoration of the Irish forms, where practicable, and he was constantly making experiments to that end. Instances of the length to which he carried this, may be found in the 4to *Spirit of the Nation.* But he had the right to take any liberties he pleased with his own verses, and where he spoiled, could alter and amend. But the Editor could not venture to tamper to any such extent with the harmony and integrity of the poems confided to him. Accordingly, the reformation of the spelling of Irish names and places has been confined to a few of the earlier Historical Ballads, where these purely Irish forms seemed more in keeping with the subject and the scene.

As Mr. Davis contributed largely to the *Spirit of the Nation,* and to the *Ballad Poetry of Ireland,* it is necessary to state here, that there are more than Thirty Poems in this volume which have not been included in any previous collection.

T. W.

INTRODUCTION.

BY THE EDITOR.

———◆———

IT is my sincere belief, that no book has ever been published, of more immediate and permanent interest to the Irish People, than this little volume of the POEMS of THOMAS DAVIS.

The momentary grief of the people for his loss was loud and ardent enough. I have heard some touching instances of the intensity with which it manifested itself in thousands, who had never seen his face, or heard his voice,—to whom, indeed, his very name and being were unknown, until the tidings of his death awoke in them the vain regret that they had not earlier known and honoured the good great man who worked unseen among them.

But, alas! regrets of this description are in their very nature transient; and all ranks of the people have much to learn before they can rightly appreciate what a treasure of hope and energy, of life and love, of greatness and glory for himself and them, lies buried in that untimely grave.

It has been the peculiar destiny of this Nation of Sorrows, to lose by unseasonable death, at the very crisis of her peril, the only men who were endowed with the genius and energy to guide her unharmed through the strife. Too seldom have Ireland's champions lived to reap the mature fruit of their toil. Too seldom hath the calm evening of existence, o'ercanopied by victory, and smiled on by such parting twilight as promises a brighter morrow, heralded for them that glad repose, which they only know who have laboured and seen their labour blessed. The insidious angel of Death has preferred to take our chieftains unprepared in their noon of manhood,—too often before that noon arrived, stabbing them stealthily in their tents, as they donned their armour, at the dawn of some great day, or mused upon the event of that encounter, which they had bent every energy to meet, and yet were doomed never to see.

Long centuries hath the hand of God, for inscrutable causes, been very heavy on Ireland; and this alacrity of Death is the fetter-key of his wrath. May this last offering of our first-born propitiate him, and may the kingly souls whom hereafter He may send among us to rule and guide our people, no more be prematurely summoned away, in the very dawn of their glory, with their hopes unrealized, and their mission unfulfilled.

Fortunately, DAVIS was not a statesman and political leader merely, but a thinker and a writer too,—more than that, a genuine poet; as, I trust, all who peruse this little book will acknowledge. True, it is a mere garland of blossoms, whose fruit was doomed never to ripen; a reliquary of undeveloped genius, but recently awakened to a consciousness of its own power.

The ambition, the activity, and above all, the overweening confidence of most young men of genius, secures for them a spontaneous discipline in those pursuits for which they are specially adapted. Goethe and Schiller, Burns and Byron, Wordsworth and Coleridge, too young as most of them were, when they commenced a career of authorship, had written verses for years before they became known to the public. Many are the recounted instances of precocious poetic power, both in those, who afterwards became renowned as poets, and in men destined to shine in far other pursuits, the first exercise of whose intellectual energy has taken this direction. Even men who, like

Cowper and Alfieri, have burst the shell of seclusion at comparatively a late period of life, have betrayed in their boyish tastes, or habits, the peculiar bent of their genius. However waywardness or timidity may have retarded the public profession of their art, they had yet some forecast of their destiny. They knew they had wings, and fluttered them, though they had not yet strength to fly.

The case of DAVIS is different, and altogether so peculiar, that it ought not to be passed over in the very briefest introduction to his poetical remains. Until about three years before his death, as I am assured, he had never written a line of poetry. His efforts to acquire knowledge, to make himself useful, and to find a suitable sphere of action, were incessant; but they tried every path, and took every direction but this. The warmth of his affections, and his intense enjoyment of the beauties of nature and character, of literature and art, ought early to have marked him out as one destined to soar and sing, as well as to think and act. But the fact is, that among his youthful cotemporaries, for many a long year, he got as little credit for any promise this way, as he did for any other remarkable qualities, beyond extreme goodnature, untiring industry, and very varied learning.

Truth to say, much of this early misconception of his character was DAVIS's own fault. He learned much; suffered much, I have no doubt; felt and sympathised much; and hoped and enjoyed abundantly; but he had not yet learned to rely on himself. His powers were like the nucleus of an embryo star, uncompressed, unpurified, flickering and indistinct. He carried about with him huge loads of what other men, most of them statists and logicians, had thought proper to assert; but what he thought and felt himself, he did not think of putting forward. The result was, that during his college course, and for some years after, while he was very generally liked, he had, unless perhaps, with some who knew him intimately, but a moderate reputation for high ability of any kind. In his twenty-fifth year, as I remember—that is, in the spring of 1839,—he first began to break out of this. His opinions began to have weight, and his character and influence to unfold themselves in a variety of ways. In the following year he entered political life. But this is not the place to recount the details of his subsequent career.

The outbreak of his poetical power began in this wise. In the autumn of 1842, taking an active part in the establishment of a new popular journal, (the *Nation*,) which was intended to advance the cause of Nationality by all the aids, which literary as well as political talent could bring to its advocacy, DAVIS, and the friends associated with him, found that while their corps in other respects was sufficiently complete, they had but scanty promise of support in the poetical department. The well-known saying of Fletcher of Saltoun,—"Give me the ballads, and let who will make the laws,"—had sunk deeply into the minds of some of the projectors of the journal: though I am told that DAVIS himself was at first not very solicitous on this point; so little aware was he of his own power in that respect, at the moment it was about to break forth. But the editor of the journal had set his heart on it, having before partially tried the experiment in a Northern paper. Ultimately, however, all the founders of the *Nation* agreed in the resolve, that come whence it would,—poetry—real living poetry, gushing warm from the heart, and not mechanically mimicking obsolete and ungenial forms,—was worth a trial, as a fosterer of National feeling, and an excitement to National hope. But it came not from any outward source; and thereupon DAVIS and his companions resolved, in default of other aid, to write the poetry themselves. They did so; they surprised themselves and everybody else. The result of that despairing attempt have since been made known, and applauded in every quarter of the globe. The right chord had been struck, and the consequent stimulus to Irish literature has been, and is incalculable.

The rapidity and thrilling power, with which, from the time that he got full access to the public ear, DAVIS developed his energies as statesman, political writer, and poet, has been well described elsewhere. It excited the surprise and admiration even of those who knew him best, and won the respect of numbers, who from political or personal prejudices, had been originally most unwilling to admit his worth. So signal a victory over long-continued neglect and obstinate prejudice as he had at length obtained, has never come under my observation, and I beleive it to be unexampled. There is no assurance of greatness so unmistakable as this. No power is so overwhelming, no energy so untiring, no enthusiasm so indomitable as that which slumbers for years, unconscious and unsuspected, until the character is completely formed, and then bursts at once into light and life, when the time for action is come.

This was the true guarantee of DAVIS's greatness—of a genius which was equal to any emergency, which would have been constantly placing itself in new aspects, overcoming new difficulties, and winning fresh love and honour from his countrymen, and from mankind. A character so rich in promise, so full of life and energy, of love and hope, as his, and at at a time so suited for public life, is a rarity in history. Had he been spared for a few years longer the world would have known this well. As it is, they must partly take it on trust from those who knew the man. For none of his writings, either in prose or verse, will enable them to know him thoroughly. As, indeed, the richer and deeper, and more vital and versatile a man's character is, the poorer fragment of himself will his writings inevitably be.

Not, but that everything DAVIS has written, abounds in admonition and instruction, for Irishmen of every class, and for all in any country who have the sympathies and affections of men. But from the activity of his public life, it was impossible that he could write with that leisure and deliberate care, which the heart and intellect require for finished composition. And accordingly, none of his works can be taken as an adequate expression of his creative power. Had he lived, and been enabled to shift a portion of his political burthen upon other shoulders, I have no doubt but he would have more frequently retired into himself, and thus been enabled to give the world the purer fruits of his unincumbered leisure. But the weight of his toil cut him off before that leisure came.

If anywhere, it is in this volume that a key to DAVIS's most engaging qualities, and to his inward heart, may be found. But there is not room here, and I must await some other opportunity of weighing the merits of these poems, in relation to their author's character, and to the wants of the time and country for which they were written. It may, at all events, be better done when his prose works also have been given to the public, and the *elite* of the labours of his young statesmanship made permanently and universally accessible. For literary pre-eminence was not his ambition at all, and even usefulness through the channels of literature, but one of the many means which he shaped to one great end.

For these and other reasons, apart from his want of leisure and his early death, his poems above all must not be judged without a reference to his aims and his mode of life. I do not believe that since the invention of printing, there has been any volume of such sincere effect and varied power, produced under similar circumstances. The longer portion and by far the best of them, were written and published in a single year (1844), and that the most active of the author's life, during which his political labours, in addition to constant writing for the journal with which he was connected, were almost as incessant and fatiguing as those of a minister of state.

In the.e and in some not dissimilar instances which I c uld recount of others, there seems good reason to hope for our country and our age. Novalis used to lament bitterly the severance of poetry from philosophy, and surely not without abundant cause ; but with far better reason might he have bemoaned the divorce of poetry from life and action. For in no respect is there a greater contrast between these latter formalized ages, and the wilder, healthier centuries of the world's antique life. Solon was a poet, as well as a statesman and sage. Sophocles was not only an unrivalled dramatist, but a distinguished soldier, and in youth a miracle of beauty and accomplishments—the Sidney as well as the Shakespeare of that glorious age. Pericles and Cæsar were orators, philosophers, soldiers, wits, poets, and consummate statesmen, all in one. Descending to a later age, entirely different in character and aims, we find Alfred teaching his people as well as ruling them. Richard Cœur-de-lion was hardly less renowned for poetry than for courage. Bertrand de Born was warrior and patriot, poet and statesman, and it was not found that his success in one pursuit was marred or defeated by his proficiency in another. Among the Moslem cotemporaries of all these men, abundant examples might be adduced of such a combination of political with poetical power. And recurring to the early dwellers in the East, above all those whom a peculiar dispensation set apart from other men, Moses and David were poets, as well as prophets and kings.

For such is the natural condition of health, in nations as in men. The mind and the body alike are agile for a thousand feats, and equal to a thousand labours. For literature is then a part of life, a dweller in the common landscape, a presence in sunshine and shade, in camp and festival, before the altar and beside the hearth,—and not an intruding reminiscence, an antiquated mockery, a ghastly effete excrescence, hiding with its bloated bulk the worth of the present hour, and the lovely opportunities of

B

unused actual life, that ever lie with mute appeal before
the dullard man ; and which he alone who feels the force
of, can enter into the feelings or appreciate the worth of
bye-gone generations too.

It is only the insidious materialism of modern existence,
that has rent the finest tissues of moral power, and dwarfed
into mechanical routine and huxtering subserviency, the
interchanging faculties of man, making literature itself a
statute-book, or a gin-shop, instead of an overhanging
canopy of the simple and sublime, a fostering, embrac-
ing atmosphere to man's every thought and act.
And thus it is that poets and philosophers,—that is, men
of purer, deeper, more genial and generative faculty than
others, -- find all the avenues to power barred against them
by lawyers and diplomatists, and are driven to suck their
thumbs in corners, when they ought, by virtue of the
fiercer life and more powerful reason that is in them, to be
teaching the world by example as well as precept ; and
not by words alone. but by the action too, by the commu-
nities of peril, and the interchange of sympathy and love,
to be filling the souls of men with hope and resolution, with
piety and truth.

Here at least, in this little book, is a precedent and admonition to the honest man-of-letters of whatever class or
country—that if his feelings for his fellow-men—and who
will feel for them, if he does not ?—should lead him into
political action, he need not despond because he is a poet,
if only he is, into the bargain, a self-reliant man. DAVIS
was a poet, but he was not for that the less practical in
public life, nor did the most prosaic of his opponents ever
object to him, that he was the less fitted to advise and
govern, because he occasionally expressed in verse the
purer aspirations of his soul.

Pity it is, to be sure, that these aspirations had not found
a fuller utterance, before the fiat of death had hushed to un-
reasonable rest the throbbings of that large heart.

Fragments though they be of a most capacious and diversified character, they are yet to a wonderful degree its unaffected utterance. Like wild flowers springing from the mould in the clefts of a giant oak, they relish of the open air, and have looked the sky in the face. Doubtless in many ways the impress of the poet's spirit, and the graces of his character, is but the purer for this partial and too late development of its loveliest folds. Like the first fragrance of the rose, ere its perfume becomes heavy with sweetness; or as the violet smells the sweetest, when hidden by its cherishing leaves from the glare of the noon-day sun.

Moreover, the supreme worth of books is as an index of character; as a fragmentary insight into unfathomed worth and power. For the man who is not better than his books, has ever seemed to me a poor creature.—Many there are, no doubt,—men whose names are high in literature—who fail to produce on their cotemporaries or on those who know their biography, an impression adequate to the promise of their writings—and some, perhaps, who really have no corresponding inward worth. Allowing for the too ardent expectations of their admirers, this indicates ever some lamentable deficiency. One cannot help occasionally, in moments of ill humour, suspecting some of these authors to be paltry second-hand thieves of other men's thoughts, or mimics of other men's energy, and not as all good writers ought to be, natural, self-taught, self-directed men. And, therefore, in honest writing, above all things, it is true, that "well begun, is half done;" be it but *once well* begun. Goldsmith's lovely nature is as visible, and more distinct in the little volume of the *Vicar of Wakefield*, than if he had written a dozen Waverly novels; *Rosamund Gray*, and *Undine* are a purer offspring of their author's minds, and a more convincing evidence of their worth, than any congeries of romances could have been.

And thus, perhaps, after all, the soul of DAVIS will shine from this book, as pure and clear,—though not so bright, or comprehensive, or beneficent,—as if he had been thirty years writing instead of three, and filled a dozen volumes instead of one. Ah! as far as writing goes there is enough to make men love him, and guess at him—and what more can the best of readers do with the supremest writer, though he lived to the age of Sophocles or Goethe. The true loss is of the oak's timber, the living tree itself, and not of its acorns or of the flowers at its base. The loss of his immediate influence on the events of his time, and on the souls of his contemporaries by guidance and example,—that is the true bereavement ; one which possibly many generations to come will be suffering from and expiating, consciously or unconsciously. So complete an endowment as his is a rare phenomenon, and no calamity can be compared with untimely extinction.

Undoubtedly the circumstances which attended the development of DAVIS's powers, are a striking proof of the latent energy which lies hid among our people, unwrought and almost unthought of. Not that I entertain the opinion, though it is a favourite theory with some men,—and one which does not obtain the less acceptance because it flatters human nature,—that there is an abundance of great men, ever walking the earth, utterly unconscious of their power, and only wanting a sufficient stimulus, themselves to know their power, and make all men acknowledge it. A theory of life and history, in any high sense of greatness, to which I cannot assent : for it seems to me the very essence of the great man is, that he is, in spite of himself, making ever new acquaintance with the realities of life. All animate and inanimate nature is in a conspiracy to make him know himself, or at least to make others know him, and by their love or hate, their fear or reverence, to awaken his slumbering might. Destiny has a thousand electric shocks in store for him, to which unearnest men are insensible ; while his own unhasting yet unresting spirit is ever fathoming new depths in the infinities of thought, and suffering, and love. For, as the wisest of the ancients told the clods who condemned him,—the great man is not born of a stock or a stone : but nature's wants are strong in him, and the ties of heart and home are as dear, or dearer to him than to any. And home is the great teacher, in childhood by its joys, in manhood by its sorrows, in age by its ebbing regrets.

No matter, then, whether thought or passion have the mastery in the great man's nature, no matter whether action or reception preponderates in his life, if he be truly great, and live through man's estate, he will in some way be recognised. Strange it were indeed, if every other element in nature—the paltriest grain of sand, or the most fleeting wave of light—were perpetual and unlimited in its influence, and the mightiest power of all, the plenitude of spiritual life, could remain unfelt by kindred spirit, for the natural life of man. True, the great man will often shun society, and court obscurity and solitude ; but let him with-draw into himself ever so much, his soul will only expand the more with thought and passion. The mystery of life will be the greater to him, the more time he has to study it ; the loveliness of nature will be the sweeter to him, the less his converse with her is disturbed by the thoughtless comment of the worldly or the vain. Let him retire into utter solitude, and even if he were not great, that solitude, —if nature whispers to him, and he listens to her,—would go near to make him so : as Selkirk, when after his four years' solitude, he trod again the streets of London, looked for a while a king, and talked like a philosopher. For a while,—since, as Richard Steele ably tells the story, in six months or so, the royalty had faded from his face, and he had grown again, what he was at first, a sturdy but common-place sailor.

But nature herself haunts incessantly the really great man, and nothing can vulgarize *him*.   And if it were only on that account alone, whether tested by action, or untested by it, the great man is sure of recognition, if allowed to live out his life.   If he act, his acts will show him ; and even if he do not act, his thoughts or his goodness will betray him.   "Hide the thoughts of such a man," says a sage of our time : "hide the sky and stars, hide the sun and moon !   Thought is all light, and publishes itself to the universe.   It will speak, though you were dumb, by some miraculous organ.   It will flow out of your actions, your manners, and your face.   It will bring you friendships, and impledge you to nature and truth, by the love and expectations of generous minds."

And yet there is in many of the best and greatest men, a tardiness of growth, which either beneficially shrouds their budding graces from the handling of impatient friends; or, at least, sets at naught that impatience, and baffs the scrutiny of the interested watcher by perpetual new growth of mere leaves, instead of the flowers and fruit he craves. Even where the natural tendency is to active life, such men will for years evince an awkwardness, a shiftlessness, an indirectness of aim, and unsteadiness of pursuit,—on the whole a hulking, slobbery ponderousness, as of an over-grown school-boy,—which will make men tardy in acknow-ledging their worth and power, when, at length, after abundant waywardness, their discipline is complete, their character formed, and their strength matured.

As to the causes of all this, I dare not enter on them now.   They all centre in a good-natured simplicity, an infantine acquiescence and credulity, which makes such slow-growing men content to be hewers of wood and drawers of water for half a life-time, until their patience is exhausted ; or until the trumpet call of duty, ever on the watch to startle them, rouses them into life ; then, at length, they commence their labours and assert their rights. In their experiences likewise, they are sometimes tardy, and as some ancient wrote, and Gœthe was fond of quoting :—

'Ο μὴ δαρεὶς ἄνθρωπος οὐ παιδεύεται.

In some such frame may the history of Davis's mind be set.

But though great men, wise men, kingly men, cannot but be few, good men and true need not be so scarce as they are,—men, I mean, true to their own convictions, and prompt in their country's need,—not greedy of distinction, but knowing well the hived sweetness that abides in an unnoticed life,—and yet not shrinking from responsibility, or avoiding danger, when the hour of trial comes. It is such men that this country needs, and not flaunting histrionists, or empty, platform patriots. She wants men who can and will work as well as talk. Men glad to live, and yet prepared to die. For Ireland is approaching her majority, and what she wants is men.

And thus is it, above all, in the manliness of this book, and of the author's character, that the germ abides of hope for the country, and of consolation for his loss. If such worth could grow up, and such success be won, amid all the treacherous influences that sap the strength of Ireland, what have we not a right to hope for? What may not be yet the glory and gladness of that distant time, when our National Genius shall at length stand regenerated and disenthralled from the shackles of foreign thought, and the contagion of foreign example; when beneath his own skies, with his own hills around, and the hearts of a whole people echoing his passionate words, he shall feel therein a content and exultation which mere cosmopolitan greatness is doomed never to know; when satisfied with ministering to the wants of the land that bore him, and having few or no affections beyond the blue waves which are its eternal boundary, he shall find his only and most ample reward in the gratitude and love of our own fervent people?

Ah ! some few short years ago, who could look for such a result with confidence? Though some there were, whom strong affections made strong in hope, that never despaired, in the gloomiest season. Times are altered since then. The eyes of our people are opened, and their hearts are changed. A swift and a surprising, and yet an easy change, for a nation perisheth not except by its own sentence. Blind though it be, it needs but be led towards the East and turned to the rising sun, Tiresias-like, to recover its sight.

Well, until a spirit of Nationality had arisen in the land and spread from sea to sea, and was not only talked of, but became an abiding principle in our lives, how could we hope to have a manly look, or a manly being among us? Or, was it that the man and the feeling both arose together, like a high-tide with a storm at its back? What else but the fostering breath of Nationality could make that genius strong, which, without such sympathy and cherishing, must necessarily grow up a weakling? For sympathy, given and received, is the life and soul of genius : without such support it crawls along — a crippled abortion, when it ought to walk abroad a giant and champion of men. Until we had proved ourselves worthy of having great men among us ; until we had shewed respect unto our dead, and taken the memory of our forgotten brave unto our hearts again, and, bid them live there for ever ; until we dared to love and honour our own, as they deserved to be loved and honoured, what had we, the Irish People, a right to expect? what goodness or greatness could we presume to claim? Until all sects and parties had at least begun to hold out a helping hand to each other, and to bind their native land with one bond of labour and love, what grace could even Nature's bounty bestow on such a graceless people?

Time was, as many alive will remember—and I have been often pained by the feeling—when, if the report of any new genius arose among us, we had to make up our minds to

find much of its brightest promise blighted in the early bud,
or stunted in maturer growth, by the mingled chill of exotic
culture and of home neglect. In those days we could never
approach a product of the National Mind, without a cold
fear at our hearts, that we should find it unworthy of the
Nation ; that we should find on it the stamp of the slave,
or the slimy trail of the stranger. And even as we gazed
with fondness and admiration on those, who in our evil days
had yet achieved something for us, and given us something
to be proud of, we still expected to meet in them some
failure, some inconsistency, some sad, some lamentable
defect, and to see the strong man totter like a weakling and
a slave.

And otherwise it could not be, in our abandonment
both of our rights, and hope to recover them. Could
the orphaned heart of genius be glad like his who had a
parent—a mother-country, a father-land? Could he who
had no country, or doubted what country he belonged to,
and knew not anything that he should care to live or die
for ; or if he dreamed of such an object, had chosen sect
instead of country—could he be strong in filial might,
and firm in manly rectitude, and bold in genial daring,
or can he yet be so among us, like him upon whose childish
thought no party spite had shed its venom, the milk of
whose untried affections sectarian hate hath curdled not ;
but the greatness and glory of his country illumined for him
the morning horizon of life ; while home, and love, and
freedom, the sovereign graces of earth, have blended in one
religion, and strengthened his heart with a mighty strength,
and chastening his spirit for ever, have made the memory
of his young days, indeed ineffably divine? Can he love
home as home should be loved, who loves not his country
too? Can he love country right, who hath no home?
Can he love home or country perfectly, to whose aching
heart the balm of love hath not been timely given? Believe it not, ye sons of men !—as he ought, he cannot. As

star poiseth star in the wilderness of the illimitable heavens,
even so the charities of life sustain each other, and centre
in the spirit of God, and bind all created beings beneath the
shelter of his love.

But enough ; a better and a brighter day is dawning,
and the

> " —— flecked darkness like a drunkard reels
> " From forth day's pathway, made by FREEDOM's wheels·"

And our lost THOMAS DAVIS was our Phosphoros, or bringer
of light !

> " Justice and Truth their winged child have fonnd!"

But let us not be incautiously hopeful.   Let us remember
that the pestilential influences, which Davis, like all of us,
had to struggle with and overcome, are still rife among us.
Let us not deceive ourselves.   The miseries of our country
for seven centuries have had foreign causes ; but there have
been, ever from the beginning of that misery, domestic
causes too.   We were divided, and did hate each other ;
and therefore we cannot stand.   It is in many respects, too,
an ill time, in which we are to unlearn these errors, and
abjure this vice, if ever we abjure it.   But He who sent the
disease will send the healing too.   Ah, why were we not
reconciled among ourselves, in earlier, in better times than
these ?   The fruit of our reconciliation then would have
been greater far than ever it can be now.   Our native laws,
and institutions, and language, were not then withered
away.   The trees which our forefathers planted, had yet
firm root in the land.   But now, in the old age of our
Nation, we had to begin life again, and with deliberate
effort, and the straining of every nerve, to repeat those toils,
which the gladness of youth made light for our fathers long
ages ago.   And this autumn blossom of our glory may go,
too, as tribute to swell the renown of those who so long
enslaved us.   Yet it is the best we can do.   There are
millions who have not food.   Are they never to be filled ?
Happy are you, after all, O youth of Ireland ! fortunate if

you but knew it, for if ever a generation had, in hope, some-thing worth living for, and in sacrifice, something worth dying for, that blessed lot is yours.

And here, youth of Ireland! in this little book is a Psalter of Nationality, in which every aspiration of your hearts will meet its due response, your every aim and effort, encouragement and sympathy, and wisest admonition. High were the hopes of our young poet patriot, and unfore-seen by him and all the stroke of fate which was to call him untimely away. The greater need that you should discipline and strengthen your souls, and bring the aid of many, to what the genius of him who is gone might have contributed more than all. Hive up strength and know-ledge. Be straightforward, and sincere, and resolute, and undismayed as he was; and God will yet reward your truth and love, and bless the land whose sons you boast your-selves to be.

T. W.

20th April, 1846.

To the Memory of Thomas Davis.

BY JOHN FISHER MURRAY.

When on the field where freedom bled,
    I press the ashes of the brave,
Marvelling that man should ever dread
    Thus to wipe out the name of slave ;
No deep-drawn sigh escapes my breast—
    No woman's drops my eyes distain,
I weep not gallant hearts at rest—
    I but deplore they died in vain.

When I the sacred spot behold,
    For aye remembered and renowned,
Where dauntless hearts and arms as bold,
    Strewed tyrants and their slaves around ;
High hopes exulting fire my breast—
    High notes triumphant swell my strain,
Joy to the brave ! in victory blest—
    Joy ! joy ! they perished not in vain.

But when thy ever mournful voice,
    My country, calls me to deplore
The champion of thy youthful choice,
    Honoured, revered, but seen no more ;
Heavy and quick my sorrows fall
    For him who strove, with might and main,
To leave a lesson for us all,
    How we might live—nor live in vain.

If, moulded of earth's common clay,
  Thou had'st to sordid arts stooped down,
Thy glorious talent flung away,
  Or sold for price thy great renown ;
In some poor pettifogging place,
  Slothful, inglorious, thou had'st lain,
Herding amid the unhonoured race,
  Who doze, and dream, and die in vain,

A spark of HIS celestial fire,
  The GOD of freemen struck from thee ;
Made thee to spurn each low desire,
  Nor bend the uncompromising knee ;
Made thee to vow thy life, to rive
  With ceaseless tug, th' oppressor's chain ;
With lyre, with pen, with sword, to strive
  For thy dear land—nor strive in vain.

How hapless is our country's fate—
  If Heaven in pity to us send
Like thee, one glorious, good, and great—
  To guide, instruct us, and amend :
How soon thy honoured life is o'er—
  Soon Heaven demandeth thee again ;
We grope on darkling as before,
  And fear lest thou hast died in vain.

In vain—no, never! O'er thy grave,
  Thy spirit dwelleth in the air ;
Thy passionate love, thy purpose brave,
  Thy hope assured, thy promise fair.
Generous and wise, farewell !—Forego
  Tears for the glorious dead and gone ;
His tears, if tears are *his*, still flow
  For slaves and cowards living on.

PART I.

NATIONAL BALLADS AND SONGS.

"NATIONAL POETRY is the very flowering of the soul – the greatest evidence of its health, the greatest excellence of its beauty. Its melody is balsam to the senses. It is the playfellow of Childhood, ripens into the companion of Manhood, consoles Age. It presents the most dramatic events, the largest characters, the most impressive scenes, and the deepest passions, in the language most familiar to us. It magnifies and ennobles our hearts, our intellects, our country, and our countrymen—binds us to the land by its condensed and gem-like history; to the future by example and by aspiration. It solaces us in travel, fires us in action, prompts our invention, sheds a grace beyond the power of luxury round our homes, is the recognised envoy of our minds among all mankind, and to all time."—*Davis's Essays.*

PART I.

NATIONAL BALLADS AND SONGS.

TIPPERARY.

I.

Let Britain boast her British hosts,
　About them all right little care we ;
Not British seas nor British coasts
　Can match the Man of Tipperary !

II.

Tall is his form, his heart is warm,
　His spirit light as any fairy—
His wrath is fearful as the storm
　That sweeps the Hills of Tipperary !

III.

Lead him to fight for native land,
　His is no courage cold and wary ;
The troops live not on earth would stand
　The headlong charge of Tipperary !

c

IV.

Yet meet him in his cabin rude,
   Or dancing with his dark-haired Mary,
You'd swear they knew no other mood
   But Mirth and Love in Tipperary!

V.

You're free to share his scanty meal,
   His plighted word he'll never vary—
In vain they tried with gold and steel
   To shake the Faith of Tipperary!

VI.

Soft is his *cailin's* sunny eye,
   Her mien is mild, her step is airy,
Her heart is fond, her soul is high—
   Oh! she's the Pride of Tipperary!

VII.

Let Britain brag her motley rag;
   We'll lift the Green more proud and airy—
Be mine the lot to bear that flag,
   And head the Men of Tipperary!

VIII.

Though Britain boasts her British hosts,
   About them all right little care we—
Give us, to guard our native coasts,
   The matchless Men of Tipperary!

THE RIVERS.

AIR—*Kathleen O'More.*

I.

'THERE's a far-famed Blackwater that runs to Loch
　　Neagh ;
'There's a fairer Blackwater that runs to the sea—
　　　The glory of Ulster,
　　　The beauty of Munster,
　　　　These twin rivers be.

II.

From the banks of that river Benburb's towers arise ;
'This stream shines as bright as a tear from sweet eyes ;
　　　This fond as a young bride,
　　　That with foeman's blood dyed—
　　　　Both dearly we prize.

III.

Deep sunk in that bed is the sword of Monroe,
Since, 'twixt it and Oonagh, he met Owen Roe,
　　　And Charlemont's cannon
　　　Slew many a man on
　　　　These meadows below.

IV.

The shrines of Armagh gleam far over yon lea,
'Nor afar is Dungannon that nursed liberty,
　　　And yonder Red Hugh
　　　Marshal Bagenal o'erthrew
　　　　On Béal-an-atha-Buidhe.*

---

* *Vulgo* Ballanabwee—the mouth of the yellow ford.

V.

But far kinder the woodlands of rich Convamore,
And more gorgeous the turrets of saintly Lismore ;
  There the stream, like a maiden
  With love overladen,
   Pants wild on each shore.

VI.

Its rocks rise like statues, tall, stately, and fair,
And the trees, and the flowers, and the mountains, and
  air,
  With Wonder's soul near you,
  To share with, and cheer you,
   Make Paradise there.

VII.

I would rove by that stream, ere my flag I unrolled ;
I would fly to these banks my betrothed to enfold—
  The pride of our sire-land,
  The Eden of Ireland,
   More precious than gold.

VIII.

May their borders be free from oppression and blight
May their daughters and sons ever fondly unite—
  The glory of Ulster,
  The beauty of Munster,
   Our strength and delight.

GLENGARIFF.

Air—O'Sullivan's March.

I.

I WANDERED at Eve by Glengariff's sweet water,
  Half in the shade, and half in the moon,
And thought of the time when the Sacsanach slaughter
  Reddened the night and darkened the noon ;
Mo nuar ! mo nuar ! mo nuar ! * I said—
    When I think, in this valley and sky—
    Where true lovers and poets should sigh—
Of the time when its chieftain O'Sullivan fled.

II.

Then my mind went along with O'Sullivan marching
  Over Musk'ry's moors and Ormond's plain,
His *curachs* the waves of the Shannon o'erarching
  And his pathway mile-marked with the slain :
Mo nuar ! mo nuar ! mo nuar ! I said—
    Yet 'twas better far from you to go,
    And to battle with torrent and foe,
Than linger as slaves where your sweet waters spread.

III.

But my fancy burst on, like a clan o'er the border,
  To times that seemed almost at hand,
When grasping her banner, old Erin's *Lamh Laidir*
  Alone shall rule over the rescued land :
O baotho ! O baotho ! O baotho ! † I said—
    Be our marching as steady and strong,
    And freemen our valleys shall throng,
'When the last of our foemen is vanquished and fled !

---

* Alas!   † Oh, fine.

THE WEST'S ASLEEP.

Air—*The Brink of the White Rocks.*

I.

WHEN all beside a vigil keep,
The West's asleep, the West's asleep—
Alas! and well may Erin weep,
When Connaught lies in slumber deep.
There lake and plain smile fair and free,
'Mid rocks—their guardian chivalry—
Sing oh! let man learn liberty
From crashing wind and lashing sea.

II.

That chainless wave and lovely land
Freedom and Nationhood demand—
Be sure, the great God never planned,
For slumbering slaves, a home so grand.
And, long, a brave and haughty race
Honoured and sentinelled the place—
Sing oh! not even their sons' disgrace
Can quite destroy their glory's trace.

III.

For often, in O'Connor's van,
To triumph dashed each Connaught clan—
And fleet as deer the Normans ran
Through Corliou's Pass and Ardrahan.
And later times saw deeds as brave;
And glory guards Clanricarde's grave—
Sing oh! they died their land to save,
At Aughrim's slopes and Shannon's wave.

IV.

And if, when all a vigil keep,
The West's asleep, the West's asleep—
Alas ! and well may Erin weep,
That Connaught lies in slumber deep.
But, hark ! some voice like thunder spake :
" *The West's awake ! the West's awake !*"—
"Sing oh ! hurra ! let England quake,
We'll watch till death for Erin's sake !"

OH ! FOR A STEED.

I.

Oh ! for a steed, a rushing steed, and a blazing sci-
mitar,
To hunt from beauteous Italy the Austrian's red
hussar ;
To mock their boasts,
And strew their hosts,
And scatter their flags afar.

II.

Oh ! for a steed, a rushing steed, and dear Poland
gathered around,
To smite her circle of savage foes, and smash them
upon the ground ;
Nor hold my hand
While, on the land,
A foreigner foe was found.

III.

Oh! for a steed, a rushing steed, and a rifle that
    never failed,
And a tribe of terrible prairie men, by desperate
    valour mailed.
      Till "stripes and stars,"
      And Russian czars,
    Before the Red Indian quailed.

IV.

Oh! for a steed, a rushing steed, on the plains of
    Hindustan,
And a hundred thousand cavaliers, to charge like a
    single man,
      Till our shirts were red,
      And the English fled
    Like a cowardly caravan.

V.

Oh! for a steed, a rushing steed, with the Greeks at
    Marathon,
Or a place in the Switzer phalanx, when the Morat
    men swept on,
      Like a pine-clad hill,
      By an earthquake's will
    Hurled the valleys upon.

VI.

Oh! for a steed, a rushing steed, when Brian smote
    down the Dane,
Or a place beside great Aodh O'Neill, when Bagenal
    the bold was slain,
      Or a waving crest
      And a lance in rest,
    With Bruce upon Bannoch plain.

VII.

Oh ! for a steed, a rushing steed, on the Curragh of
   Kildare,
And Irish squadrons skilled to do, as they are ready
   to dare—
      A hundred yards,
      And Holland's guards
     Drawn up to engage me there.

VIII.

Oh ! for a steed, a rushing steed, and any good cause
   at all,
Or else, if you will, a field on foot, or guarding a
   leaguered wall
      For freedom's right ;
      In flushing fight
     To conquer if then to fall.

CYMRIC RULE AND CYMRIC RULERS.*

Air—*The March of the Men of Harlech.*

I.

Once there was a Cymric nation ;
Few its men, but high its station—
Freedom is the soul's creation,
   Not the work of hands.
Coward hearts are self-subduing ;
Fetters last by slaves' renewing—
Edward's castles are in ruin,
   Still his empire stands.

* *Vide* Appendix iv.

Still the Saxon's malice
Blights our beauteous valleys ;
Ours the toil, but his the spoil, and his the laws we
    writhe in ;
Worked like beasts, that Saxon priests may riot in our
    tithing ;
      Saxon speech and Saxon teachers
        Crush our Cymric tongue !
      Tolls our traffic binding,
      Rents our vitals grinding—
Bleating sheep, we cower and weep, when, by one bold
    endeavour,
We could drive from out our hive these Saxon drones
    for ever.
      "CYMRIC RULE AND CYMRIC RULERS"—
        Pass along the word !

          II.

      We should blush at Arthur's glory—
      Never sing the deeds of Rory—
      Caratach's renowned story
        Deepens our disgrace.
      By the bloody day of Banchor !
      By a thousand years of rancour !
      By the wrongs that in us canker !
        Up ! ye Cymric race—
      Think of Old Llewellyn—
      Owen's trumpets swelling ;
Then send out a thunder shout, and every true man
    summon,
Till the ground shall echo round from Severn to Plin-
    limmon,

"Saxon foes and Cymric brothers,
    "Arthur's come again !"
Not his bone and sinew,
But his soul within you,
Prompt and true to plan and do, and firm as Mon-
    mouth iron,
For our cause, though crafty laws and charging troops
    environ—
        CYMBRIC RULE AND CYMBRIC RULERS "—
        Pass along the word !

A BALLAD OF FREEDOM.

I.

THE Frenchman sailed in Freedom's name to smite
    the Algerine,
The strife was short, the crescent sunk, and then his
    guile was seen ;
For, nestling in the pirate's hold—a fiercer pirate far—
He bade the tribes yield up their flocks, the towns
    their gates unbar.
Right on he pressed with freemen's hands to subjugate
    the free,
The Berber in old Atlas glens, the Moor in Titteri ;
And wider had his *razzias* spread, his cruel conquests
    broader,
But God sent down, to face his frown, the gallant
    Abdel-Kader—
The faithful Abdel-Kader ! unconquered Abdel-Kader.
        Like falling rock,
        Or fierce siroc—

No savage or marauder—
Son of a slave !
First of the brave !
Hurrah for Abdel-Kader !

II.

The Englishman, for long, long years, had ravaged
Ganges' side—
A dealer first, intriguer next, he conquered far and
wide,
Till, hurried on by avarice, and thirst of endless
rule,
His sepoys pierced to Candahar, his flag waved in
Cabul ;
But still within the conquered land, was one uncon-
quered man,
The fierce Pushtani* lion, the fiery Akhbar Khan—
He slew the sepoys on the snow, till Scindh's full
flood they swam it
Right rapidly, content to flee the son of Dost Mo-
hammed,
The son of Dost Mohammed, and brave old Dost
Mohammed—
Oh ! long may they
Their mountains sway,
Akhbar and Dost Mohammed !
Long live the Dost !
Who Britain crost,
Hurrah for Dost Mohammed !

---

* This is the name by which the Affghans call themselves. Affghan
is the Persian name (see Elphinstone's delightful book on Cabul).

III.

The Russian, lord of million serfs, and nobles serflier
    still,
Indignant saw Circassia's sons bear up against his will;
With fiery ships he lines their coast, his armies cross
    their streams—
He builds a hundred fortresses—his conquests done,
    he deems.
But steady rifles—rushing steeds—a crowd of nameless
    chiefs—
The plough is o'er his arsenals;—his feet is on the reefs!
The maidens of Kabyntica are clad in Moscow dresses—
His slavish herd, how dared they beard the mountain-
    bred Cherkesses !
The lightning Cherkesses !—the thundering Cher-
    kesses !
        May Elburz top
        In Azof drop,
   Ere Cossacks beat Cherkesses !
        The fountain head
        Whence Europe spread—
  Hurrah ! for the tall Cherkesses !*

IV.

But Russia preys on Poland's fields, where Sobieski
    reigned,
And Austria on Italy—the Roman eagle chained—
Bohemia, Servia, Hungary, within her clutches, gasp;
And Ireland struggles gallantly in England's loosening
    grasp.

* Cherkesses or Abdzes is the right name of the so-called Circassians.
Kabyntica is a town in the heart of the Caucasus, of which Mount Elburz
is the summit. Blumenbach and other physiologists assert that the
finer European races descend from a Circassian stock.

Oh ! would all these their strength unite, or battle on
    alone,
Like Moor, Pushtani, and Cherkess, they soon would
    have their own.
Hurrah ! hurrah ! it can't be far, when from the Scindh
    to Shannon,
Shall gleam a line of freemen's flags begirt by free-
    men's cannon !
The coming day of Freedom—the flashing flags of
    Freedom ;
        The victor glaive—
        The mottoes brave,
    May we be there to read them !
        That glorious noon,
        God send it soon—
    Hurrah for human freedom !

THE IRISH HURRAH.

Air--*Nach m-baineann sin do.*

I.

Have you hearkened the eagle scream over the sea ;
Have you hearkened the breaker beat under your lee.
A something between the wild waves, in their play,
And the kingly bird's scream, is The Irish Hurrah.

II.

How it rings on the rampart when Saxons assail—
How it leaps on the level, and crosses the vale,
Till the talk of the cataract faints on its way,
And the echo's voice cracks with The Irish Hurrah.

III.

How it sweeps o'er the mountain when hounds are on
    scent,
How it presses the billows when rigging is rent,
Till the enemy's broadside sinks low in dismay,
As our boarders go in with The Irish Hurrah.

IV.

Oh ! there's hope in the trumpet and glee in the fife,
But never such music broke into a strife,
As when at its bursting the war-clouds give way,
And there's cold steel along with The Irish Hurrah.

V.

What joy for a death bed, your banner above,
And round you the pressure of patriot love,
As you're lifted to gaze on the breaking array
Of the Saxon reserve at The Irish Hurrah.

A SONG FOR THE IRISH MILITIA.

Air—*The Peacock.*

I.

The tribune's tongue and poet's pen
May sow the seed in prostrate men ;
But 'tis the soldier's sword alone
Can reap the crop so bravely sown !
No more I'll sing nor idly pine,
But train my soul to lead a line—
A soldier's life's the life for me—
A soldier's death, so Ireland's free !

II.

No foe would fear your thunder words,
If 'twere not for your lightning swords—
If tyrants yield when millions pray,
'Tis lest they link in war array ;
Nor peace itself is safe, but when
The sword is sheathed by fighting men—
A soldier's life 's the life for me—
A soldier's death, so Ireland's free !

III.

The rifle brown and sabre bright
Can freely speak and nobly write—
What prophets preached the truth so well
As HOFER, BRIAN, BRUCE, and TELL ?
God guard the creed these heroes taught—
That blood-bought Freedom's cheaply bought.
A soldier's life 's the life for me—
A soldier's death, so Ireland's free !

IV.

Then, welcome be the bivouac,
The hardy stand, and fierce attack,
Where pikes will tame their carbineers,
And rifles thin their bay'neteers,
And every field the island through
Will show " what Irishmen can do !"
A soldier's life 's the life for me—
A soldier's death, so Ireland's free !

V.

Yet, 'tis not strength, and 'tis not steel
Alone can make the English reel ;
But wisdom, working day by day,
Till comes the time for passion's sway—
The patient dint, and powder shock,
Can blast an empire like a rock.
A soldier's life's the life for me—
A soldier's death, so Ireland's free !

VI.

The tribune's tongue and poet's pen
May sow the seed in slavish men ;
But 'tis the soldier's sword alone
Can reap the harvest when 'tis grown.
No more I'll sing, no more I'll pine,
But train my soul to lead a line—
A soldier's life's the life for me—
A soldier's death, so Ireland's free.

OUR OWN AGAIN.

I.

LET the coward shrink aside,
    We'll have our own again ;
Let the brawling slave deride—
    Here's for our own again !
Let the tyrant bribe and lie,
March, threaten, fortify,
Loose his lawyer and his spy—
    Yet we'll have our own again !

D

Let him soothe in silken tone,
Scold from a foreign throne ;
Let him come with bugles blown—
  We shall have our own again !
Let us to our purpose bide,
  We'll have our own again !
Let the game be fairly tried,
  We'll have our own again !

II.

Send the cry throughout the land,
  " Who's for our own again ?"
Summon all men to our band,—
  Why not our own again ?
Rich, and poor, and old, and young,
Sharp sword, and fiery tongue,
Soul and sinew firmly strung—
  All to get our own again !
Brothers strive by brotherhood—
Trees in a stormy wood—
Riches come from Nationhood—
  Sha'n't we have our own again ?
Munster's woe is Ulster's bane !
  Join for our own again—
Tyrants rob as well as reign—
  We'll have our own again !

III.

Oft our fathers' hearts it stirred,
  " Rise for our own again !"
Often passed the signal word,
  " Strike for our own again !"
Rudely, rashly, and untaught,

Uprose they, ere they ought,
Failing, though they nobly fought—
　　Dying for their own again !
Mind will rule and muscle yield,
In senate, ship, and field :
When we've skill our strength to wield,
　　Let us take our own again !
By the slave his chain is wrought—
　　Strive for our own again.
Thunder is less strong than thought—
　　We'll have our own again !

IV.

Calm as granite to our foes,
　　Stand for our own again ;
Till his wrath to madness grows,
　　Firm for our own again.
Bravely hope, and wisely wait,
Toil, join, and educate ;
Man is master of his fate ;
　　We'll enjoy our own again !
With a keen constrained thirst—
Powder's calm ere it burst—
Making ready for the worst—
　　So we'll get our own again.
Let us to our purpose bide,
　　We'll have our own again !
God is on the righteous side,
　　We'll have our own again !

CELTS AND SAXONS.*

I.

WE hate the Saxon and the Dane,
 We hate the Norman men—
We cursed their greed for blood and gain,
 We curse them now again.
Yet start not, Irish-born man !
 If you're to Ireland true,
We heed not blood, nor creed, nor clan—
 We have no curse for you.

II.

We have no curse for you or your's
 But Friendship's ready grasp,
And Faith to stand by you and your's
 Unto our latest gasp—
To stand by you against all foes,
 Howe'er, or whence they come,
With traitor arts, or bribes, or blows,
 From England, France, or Rome.

III.

What matter that at different shrines
 We pray unto one God—
What matter that at different times
 Your fathers won this sod—
In fortune and in name we're bound
 By stronger links than steel ;
And neither can be safe nor sound
 But in the other's weal.

---

* Written in reply to some very beautiful verses printed in the *Evening Mail*, deprecating and defying the assumed hostility of the Irish Celts to the *Irish* Saxons.

IV.

As Nubian rocks, and Ethiop sand
   Long drifting down the Nile,
Built up old Egypt's fertile land
   For many a hundred mile ;
So Pagan clans to Ireland came,
   And clans of Christendom,
Yet joined their wisdom and their fame
   To build a nation from.

V.

Here came the brown Phœnician,
   The man of trade and toil—
Here came the proud Milesian,
   A hungering for spoil ;
And the Firbolg and the Cymry,
   And the hard, enduring Dane,
And the iron Lords of Normandy,
   With the Saxons in their train.

VI.

And oh ! it were a gallant deed
   To show before mankind,
How every race and every creed
   Might be by love combined—
Might be combined, yet not forget
   The fountains whence they rose,
As, filled by many a rivulet,
   The stately Shannon flows.

VII.

Nor would we wreak our ancient feud
　　On Belgian or on Dane,
Nor visit in a hostile mood
　　The hearths of Gaul or Spain ;
But long as on our country lies
　　The Anglo-Norman yoke,
Their tyranny we'll stigmatize,
　　And God's revenge invoke.

VIII.

We do not hate, we never cursed,
　　Nor spoke a foeman's word
Against a man in Ireland nursed,
　　Howe'er we thought he erred ;
So start not, Irish-born man,
　　If you're to Ireland true,
We heed not race, nor creed, nor clan,
　　We've hearts and hands for you.

ORANGE AND GREEN WILL CARRY THE DAY.

Air—*The Protestant Boys.*

I.

IRELAND ! rejoice, and England ! deplore—
Faction and feud are passing away.
'Twas a low voice, but 'tis a loud roar,
　　" Orange and Green will carry the day."
　　　　Orange ! Orange !
　　　　Green and Orange !
Pitted together in many a fray-

Lions in fight !
And linked in their might,
Orange and Green will carry the day.
    Orange ! Orange !
    Green and Orange !
Wave them together o'er mountain and bay.
    Orange and Green !
    Our King and our Queen !
" Orange and Green will carry the day !"

II.

Rusty the swords our fathers unsheathed—
    William and James are turned to clay—
Long did we till the wrath they bequeathed ;
    Red was the crop, and bitter the pay !
      Freedom fled us !
      Knaves misled us !
Under the feet of the foemen we lay—
      Riches and strength
      We'll win them at length,
For Orange and Green will carry the day !
      Landlords fooled us ;
      England ruled us,
Hounding our passions to make us their prey :
      But, in their spite,
      The Irish UNITE,
And Orange and Green will carry the day !

III.

Fruitful our soil where honest men starve ;
    Empty the mart, and shipless the bay ;
Out of our want the Oligarchs carve ;
    Foreigners fatten on our decay !

Disunited,
Therefore blighted,
Ruined and rent by the Englishman's sway ;
Party and creed
For once have agreed—
Orange and Green will carry the day !
Boyne's old water,
Red with slaughter !
Now is as pure as an infant at play ;
So, in our souls,
Its history rolls,
And Orange and Green will carry the day !

IV.

English deceit can rule us no more,
  Bigots and knaves are scattered like spray—
Deep was the oath the Orangeman swore,
  "Orange and Green must carry the day !"
    Orange ! Orange !
    Bless the Orange !
Tories and Whigs grew pale with dismay,
    When from the North,
    Burst the cry forth,
  "Orange and Green will carry the day ;"
    No surrender !
    No Pretender !
Never to falter and never betray—
    With an Amen,
    We swear it again,
ORANGE AND GREEN SHALL CARRY THE DAY.

"THE elements of Irish nationality are not only combining—in fact, they are growing confluent in our minds. Such nationality as merits a good man's help, and awakens a true man's ambition—such nationality as could stand against internal faction and foreign intrigue—such nationality as would make the Irish hearth happy, and the Irish name illustrious, is becoming understood. It must contain and represent all the races of Ireland. It must not be Celtic; it must not be Saxon; it must be Irish. The Brehon law, and the maxims of Westminster—the cloudy and lightning genius of the Gael, the placid strength of the Sacsanach, the marshalling insight of the Norman—a literature which shall exhibit in combination the passions and idioms of all, and which shall equally express our mind, in its romantic, its religious, its forensic, and its practical tendencies—finally, a native government, which shall know and rule by the might and right of all, yet yield to the arrogance of none—these are the components of such a nationality."—DAVIS'S ESSAYS.

"It is not a gambling fortune, made at imperial play, Ireland wants; it is the pious and stern cultivation of her faculties and her virtues, the acquisition of faithful and exact habits, and the self-respect that rewards a dutiful and sincere life. To get her peasants into snug homesteads, with well-tilled fields and placid hearths—to develope the ingenuity of her artists, and the docile industry of her artizans—to make for her own instruction a literature wherein our climate, history, and passions shall breathe—to gain conscious strength and integrity, and the high post of holy freedom—these are Ireland's wants."—Davis's Essays.

PART II.

MISCELLANEOUS SONGS AND BALLADS.

"THE greatest achievement of the Irish people is their music. It tells their history, climate, and character; but it too much loves to weep. Let us, when so many of our chains have been broken—when our strength is great, and our hopes high, cultivate its bolder strains—its raging and rejoicing; or if we weep, let it be like men whose eyes are lifted, though their tears fall.

"Music is the first faculty of the Irish; and scarcely anything has such power for good over them. The use of this faculty and this power. publicly and constantly, to keep up their spirits, refine their tastes, warm their courage, increase their union, and renew their zeal—is the duty of every patriot."—DAVIS's ESSAYS.

PART II.

MISCELLANEOUS SONGS AND BALLADS.

THE LOST PATH.

Air.—*Grádh mo chroide*

I.

SWEET thoughts, bright dreams, my comfort be,
　　All comfort else has flown ;
For every hope was false to me,
　　And here I am, alone.
What thoughts were mine in early youth !
　　Like some old Irish song,
Brimful of love, and life, and truth,
　　My spirit gushed along.

II.

I hoped to right my native isle,
　　I hoped a soldier's fame,
I hoped to rest in woman's smile,
　　And win a minstel's name—
Oh ! little have I served my land,
　　No laurels press my brow,
I have no woman's heart or hand,
　　Nor minstrel honours now.

III.

But fancy has a magic power,
 It brings me wreath and crown,
And woman's love, the self-same hour
 It smites oppression down.
Sweet thoughts, bright dreams, my comfort be,
 I have no joy beside ;
Oh ! throng around, and be to me
 Power, country, fame, and bride,

LOVE'S LONGINGS.

I.

To the conqueror his crowning,
 First freedom to the slave,
And air unto the drowning,
 Sunk in the ocean's wave—
And succour to the faithful,
 Who fight their flag above,
Are sweet, but far less grateful
 Than were my lady's love.

II.

I know I am not worthy
 Of one so young and bright ;
And yet I would do for thee
 Far more than others might ;
I cannot give you pomp or gold,
 If you should be my wife,
But I can give you love untold,
 And true in death or life.

III.

Methinks that there are passions
   Within that heaving breast
To scorn their heartless fashions,
   And wed whom you love best.
Methinks you would be prouder
   As the struggling patriot's bride,
Than if rank your home should crowd, or
   Cold riches round you glide.

IV.

Oh ! the watcher longs for morning,
   And the infant cries for light,
And the saint for heaven's warning,
   And the vanquished pray for might ;
But their prayer, when lowest kneeling,
   And their suppliance most true,
Are cold to the appealing
   Of this longing heart to you.

HOPE DEFERRED.

Air –. *Oh ! art thou gone, my Mary dear ?*

I.

'Tis long since we were forced to part, at least it seems
   so to my grief,
For sorrow wearies us like time, but ah ! it brings not
   time's relief ;
As in our days of tenderness, before me still she seems
   to glide ;

And, though my arms are wide as then, yet she will
    not abide.
The day-light and the star-light shine, as if her eyes
    were in their light,
And, whispering in the panting breeze, her love-songs
    come at lonely night ;
While, far away with those less dear, she tries to hide
    her grief in vain,
For, kind to all while true to me, it pains her to give
    pain.

II.

I know she never spoke her love, she never breathed a
    single vow,
And yet I'm sure she loved me then, and still she doats
    on me now ;
For, when we met, her eyes grew glad, and heavy
    when I left her side,
And oft she said she'd be most happy as a poor man's
    bride ;
I toiled to win a pleasant home, and make it ready by
    the spring ;
The spring is past—what season now my girl unto our
    home will bring ?
I'm sick and weary, very weary—watching, morning,
    night, and noon ;
How long you're coming—I am dying—will you not
    come soon ?

EIBHLIN A RUIN.

I.

WHEN I am far away,
 Eibhlín a rúin,
Be gayest of the gay,
 Eibhlín a rúin.
Too dear your happiness,
For me to wish it less—
Love has no selfishness,
 Eibhlín a rúin.

II.

And it must be our pride,
 Eibhlín a rúin,
Our trusting hearts to hide,
 Eibhlín a rúin.
They wish our love to blight,
We'll wait for Fortune's light—
The flowers close up at night,
 Eibhlín a rúin.

III.

And when we meet alone,
 Eibhlín a rúin,
Upon my bosom thrown,
 Eibhlín a rúin ;
That hour, with light bedecked,
Shall cheer us and direct,
A beacon to the wrecked,
 Eibhlín a rúin.

IV.

Fortune, thus sought, will come,
Eibhlín a rúin.
We'll win a happy home,
Eibhlín a rúin;
And, as it slowly rose
'Twill tranquilly repose,
A rock 'mid melting snows,
Eibhlín a rúin.

THE BANKS OF THE LEE.

Air.—*A Trip to the Cottage.*

I.

Oh! the banks of the Lee, the banks of the Lee,
And love in a cottage for Mary and me;
There's not in the land a lovelier tide,
And I'm sure there's no one so fair as my bride.
She's modest and meek,
There's a down on her cheek,
And her skin is as sleek
As a butterfly's wing—
Then her step would scarce show
On the fresh-fallen snow;
And her whisper is low,
But as clear as the spring.
Oh! the banks of the Lee, the banks of the Lee,
And love in a cottage for Mary and me:
I know not how love is happy elsewhere;
I know not how any but lovers are there!

II.

Oh ! so green is the grass, so clear is the stream,
So mild is the mist, and so rich is the beam,
That beauty should ne'er to other lands roam,
But make on the banks of the river its home.
    When, dripping with dew,
    The roses peep through,
    'Tis to look in at you
      They are growing so fast ;
    While the scent of the flowers
    Must be hoarded for hours,
    'Tis poured in such showers
      When my Mary goes past.
Oh ! the banks of the Lee, the banks of the Lee,
And love in a cottage for Mary and me—
Oh, Mary for me—oh, Mary for me !
And 'tis little I'd sigh for the banks of the Lee !

THE GIRL OF DUNBWY.

I.

'Tis pretty to see the girl of Dunbwy
Stepping the mountain statelily—
Though ragged her gown, and naked her feet,
No lady in Ireland to match her is meet.

II.

Poor is her diet, and hardly she lies—
Yet a monarch might kneel for a glance of her eyes ;
The child of a peasant—yet England's proud Queen
Has less rank in her heart, and less grace in her mien.

III.

Her brow 'neath her raven hair gleams, just as if
A breaker spread white 'neath a shadowy cliff—
And love, and devotion, and energy speak
From her beauty-proud eye, and her passion-pale cheek.

IV.

But, pale as her cheek is, there's fruit on her lip,
And her teeth flash as white as the crescent moon's tip,
And her form and her step, like the reed-deer's, go past —
As lightsome, as lovely, as haughty, as fast.

V.

I saw her but once, and I looked in her eye,
And she knew that I worshipped in passing her by ;
The saint of the wayside—she granted my prayer,
Though we spoke not a word, for her mother was there.

VI.

I never can think upon Bantry's bright hills,
But her image starts up, and my longing eye fills ;
And I whisper her softly, "again, love, we'll meet !
And I'll lie in your bosom, and live at your feet."

DUTY AND LOVE.

Air.—My lodging is on the cold ground.

I.

Oh ! lady, think not that my heart has grown cold,
    If I woo not as once I could woo ;
Though sorrow has bruised it, and long years have rolled,
    It still dotes on beauty and you :
And were I to yield to its inmost desire,
    I would labour by night and by day,
Till I won you to flee from the home of your sire,
    To live with your love far away.

II.

But it is that my country's in bondage, and I
    Have sworn to shatter her chains !
By my duty and oath I must do it or lie
    A corse on her desolate plains :
Then sure, dearest maiden, 'twere sinful to sue,
    And crueller far to win,
But, should victory smile on my banner, to you
    I shall fly without sorrow or sin.

ANNIE DEAR.

Air.—Maids in May.

I.

Our mountain brooks were rushing,
        Annie, dear,
The Autumn eve was flushing,
        Annie, dear ;

But brighter was your blushing,
When first, your murmurs hushing,
I told my love outgushing,
                    Annie, dear.

II.

Ah ! but our hopes were splendid,
                    Annie, dear,
How sadly they have ended,
                    Annie, dear ;
The ring betwixt us broken,
When our vows of love were spoken,
Of your poor heart was a token,
                    Annie, dear.

III.

The primrose flowers were shining,
                    Annie, dear,
When on my breast reclining,
                    Annie, dear !
Began our *Mi-na-meala*,
And many a month did follow
Of joy—but life is hollow,
                    Annie, dear.

IV.

For once, when home returning,
                    Annie, dear,
I found our cottage burning,
                    Annie, dear ;
Around it were the yeomen,
Of every ill an omen,
The country's bitter foemen,
                    Annie, dear.

V.

But why arose a morrow,
              Annie, dear,
Upon that night of sorrow,
              Annie, dear?
Far better, by thee lying,
Their bayonets defying,
Than live an exile sighing ;
              Annie, dear.

BLIND MARY.

AIR.—*Blind Mary.*

I.

THERE flows from her spirit such love and delight,
That the face of Blind Mary is radiant with light—
As the gleam from a homestead through darkness will
      show,
Or the moon glimmer soft through the fast falling snow.

II.

Yet there's a keen sorrow comes o'er her at times,
As an Indian might feel in our northerly climes !
And she talks of the sunset, like parting of friends,
And the starlight, as love, that nor changes nor ends.

III.

Ah ! grieve not, sweet maiden, for star or for sun,
For the mountains that tower or the rivers that run—
For beauty and grandeur, and glory, and light,
Are seen by the spirit, and not by the sight.

IV.

In vain for the thoughtless are sunburst and shade,
In vain for the heartless flowers blossom and fade ;
While the darkness that seems your sweet being to
    bound
Is one of the guardians, an Eden around !

THE BRIDE OF MALLOW.

I.

'Twas dying they thought her,
And kindly they brought her
To the banks of Blackwater,
    Where her forefathers lie ;
'Twas the place of her childhood,
And they hoped that its wild wood,
And air soft and mild would
    Soothe her spirit to die.

II.

But she met on its border
A lad who adored her—
No rich man, nor lord, or
    A coward, or slave ;
But one who had worn
A green coat, and borne
A pike from Slieve Mourne,
    With the patriots brave.

III.

Oh ! the banks of the streams are
Than emeralds greener ;
And how should they wean her
    From loving the earth ?
While the song-birds so sweet,
And the waves at their feet,
And each young pair they meet,
    Are all flushing with mirth.

IV.

And she listed his talk,
And he shared in her walk—
And how could she balk
    One so gallant and true ?
But why tell the rest ?
    Her love she confest,
And sunk on his breast,
    Like the eventide dew.

V.

Ah ! now her cheek glows
With the tint of the rose,
And her healthful blood flows,
    Just as fresh as the stream ;
And her eye flashes bright,
And her footstep is light,
And sickness and blight
    Fled away like a dream.

VI.

And soon by his side
She kneels a sweet bride,
In maidenly pride
        And maidenly fears ;
And their children were fair,
And their home knew no care,
Save that all homesteads were
        Not as happy as theirs.

THE WELCOME.

Air,—*An buachailin buidhe.*

I.

Come in the evening, or come in the morning,
Come when you're looked for, or come without warning,
Kisses and welcome you'll find here before you,
And the oftener you come here the more I'll adore you.
    Light is my heart since the day we were plighted,
    Red is my cheek that they told me was blighted ;
    The green of the trees looks far greener than ever,
    And the linnets are singing, "true lovers! don't sever.'

II.

I'll pull you sweet flowers, to wear if you choose them ;
Or, after you've kissed them, they'll lie on my bosom.
I'll fetch from the mountain its breeze to inspire you ;
I'll fetch from my fancy a tale that won't tire you.

Oh ! your step's like the rain to the summer-vexed
    farmer,
Or sabre and shield to a knight without armour :
I'll sing you sweet songs till the stars rise above me,
Then, wandering, I'll wish you, in silence, to love me.

III.

We'll look through the trees at the cliff, and the eyrie,
We'll tread round the rath on the track of the fairy,
We'll look on the stars, and we'll list to the river,
Till you ask of your darling what gift you can give her.
    Oh! she'll whisper you, "Love as unchangeably
        beaming,
    And trust, when in secret, most tunefully streaming,
    Till the starlight of heaven above us shall quiver,
    As our souls flow in one down eternity's river."

IV.

So come in the evening, or come in the morning,
Come when you're looked for, or come without warning,
Kisses and welcome you'll find here before you,
And the oftener you come here the more I'll adore you !
    Light is my heart since the day we were plighted,
    Red is my cheek that they told me was blighted ;
    The green of the trees looks far greener than ever,
    And the linnets are singing, "true lovers! don't sever!'

THE MI-NA-MEALA.*

I.

LIKE the rising of the sun,
　Herald of bright hours to follow,
Lo ! the marriage rites are done,
　And begun the *Mi-na-Meala*.

II.

Heart to heart, and hand to hand,
　Vowed 'fore God to love and cherish,
Each by each in grief to stand,
　Never more apart to flourish.

III.

Now their lips, low whisp'ring, speak
　Thoughts their eyes have long been saying,
Softly bright, and richly meek,
　As seraphs first their wings essaying.

IV.

Deeply, wildly, warmly, love—
　'Tis a heaven-sent enjoyment,
Lifting up our thoughts above
　Selfish aims and cold employment.

V.

Yet, remember, passion wanes,
　Romance is parent to dejection ;
Nought our happiness sustains
　But thoughtful care and firm affection.

* The *Honeymoon.*

VI.

When the *Mi-na-meala's* flown,
    Sterner duties surely need you ;
Do their bidding,—'tis love's own,—
    Faithful love will say God speed you.

VII.

Guard her comfort as 'tis worth,
    Pray to God to look down on her ;
And swift as cannon-shot go forth
    To strive for freedom, truth, and honour.

VIII.

Oft recall—and never swerve—
    Your children's love and her's will follow ;
Guard your home, and there preserve
    For you an endless *Mi-na-meala.*

MAIRE BHAN A STOIR.*

I.

In a valley, far away,
    With my *Máire bhán a stóir*,
Short would be the summer-day,
    Ever loving more and more ;
Winter-days would all grow long,
    With the light her heart would pour,
With her kisses and her song,
    And her loving *maith go leór.*

---

* Pronounce *Maurya rawn asthore*—that is, "Fair Mary, my treasure.'

Fond is *Máire bhán a stóir*,
Fair is *Máire bhán a stóir*,
Sweet as ripple on the shore,
Sings my *Máire bhán a stóir*.

II.

Oh! her sire is very proud,
  And her mother cold as stone;
But her brother bravely vowed
  She should be my bride alone;
For he knew I loved her well,
  And he knew she loved me too,
So he sought their pride to quell,
  But 'twas all in vain to sue.
      True is *Máire bhán a stóir*,
      Tried is *Máire bhán a stóir*,
      Had I wings I'd never soar,
      From my *Máire bhán a stóir*.

III.

There are lands where manly toil
  Surely reaps the crop it sows,
Glorious woods and teeming soil,
  Where the broad Missouri flows;
Through the trees the smoke shall rise,
  From our hearth with *maith go leór*,
There shall shine the happy eyes
  Of my *Máire bhán a stóir*.
      Mild is *Máire bhán a stóir*,
      Mine is *Máire bhán a stóir*,
      Saints will watch about the door
      Of my *Máire bhán a stóir*.

OH! THE MARRIAGE.

AIR.—*The Swaggering Jig.*

I.

OH! the marriage, the marriage,
  With love and *mo bhuachaill* for me,
The ladies that ride in a carriage
  Might envy my marriage to me;
For Eoghan* is straight as a tower,
  And tender and loving and true,
He told me more love in an hour
  Than the Squires of the county could do.
          Then, Oh! the marriage, &c.

II.

His hair is a shower of soft gold,
  His eye is as clear as the day,
His conscience and vote were unsold
  When others were carried away;
His word is as good as an oath,
  And freely 'twas given to me;
Oh! sure 'twill be happy for both
  The day of our marriage to see.
          Then, Oh! the marriage, &c.

III.

His kinsmen are honest and kind,
  The neighbours think much of his skill,
And Eoghan's the lad to my mind,
  Though he owns neither castle nor mill.

---

* *Vulgo* Owen; a name frequent among the Cymry (Welsh).

But he has a tilloch of land,
  A horse, and a stocking of coin,
A foot for a dance, and a hand
  In the cause of his country to join.
              Then, Oh ! the marriage, &c.

IV.

We meet in the market and fair—
  We meet in the morning and night—
He sits on the half of my chair,
  And my people are wild with delight.
Yet I long through the winter to skim,
  Though Eoghan longs more I can see,
When I will be married to him,
  And he will be married to me.
          Then, oh ! the marriage, the marriage,
              With love and *mo buachaill* for me,
          The ladies that ride in a carriage,
              Might envy my marriage to me.

A PLEA FOR LOVE.

I.

THE summer brook flows in the bed,
  The winter torrent tore asunder ;
The sky-lark's gentle wings are spread,
  Where walk the lightning and the thunder ;
And thus you'll find the sternest soul
  The gayest tenderness concealing,
And minds that seem to mock control,
  Are ordered by some fairy feeling.

II.

Then, maiden ! start not from the hand
  That's hardened by the swaying sabre—
The pulse beneath may be as bland
  As evening after day of labour :
And, maiden ! start not from the brow
  That thought has knit, and passion darkened—
In twilight hours, 'neath forest bough,
  The tenderest tales are often hearkened.

THE BISHOP'S DAUGHTER.

Air –*The Maid of Killala.*

I.

KILLALA's halls are proud and fair ;
Tyrawley's hills are cold and bare ;
Yet, in the palace, you were sad,
While, here, your heart is safe and glad.

II.

No satin couch, no maiden train,
Are here to soothe each passing pain ;
Yet lay your head my breast upon—
'Twill turn to down for you, sweet one !

III.

Your father's halls are rich and fair,
And plain the home you've come to share ;
But happy love's a fairy king,
And sheds a grace on every thing.

F

THE BOATMAN OF KINSALE.

AIR.—*An Cota Caol.*

I.

His kiss is sweet, his word is kind,
  His love is rich to me ;
I could not in a palace find
  A truer heart than he.
The eagle shelters not his nest
  From hurricane and hail,
More bravely than he guards my breast—
  The Boatman of Kinsale.

II.

The wind that round the Fastnet sweeps
  Is not a whit more pure—
The goat that down Cnoc Sheehy leaps
  Has not a foot more sure.
No firmer hand nor freer eye
  E'er faced an autumn gale—
De Courcy's heart is not so high—
  The Boatman of Kinsale.

III.

The brawling squires may heed him not,
  The dainty stranger sneer—
But who will dare to hurt our cot,
  When Myles O'Hea is here ?
The scarlet soldiers pass along ;
  They'd like, but fear to rail ;
His blood is hot, his blow is strong—
  The Boatman of Kinsale.

IV.

His hooker's in the Scilly van,
 When seines are in the foam ;
But money never made the man,
 Nor wealth a happy home.
So, blest with love and liberty,
 While he can trim a sail,
He'll trust in God, and cling to me—
 The Boatman of Kinsale.

DARLING NELL.

I.

WHY should not I take her unto my heart ?
She has not a morsel of guile or art ;
Why should not I make her my happy wife,
And love her and cherish her all my life ?
I've met with a few of as shining eyes ;
I've met with a hundred of wilder sighs ;
I think I met some whom I loved as well—
But none who loved me like my Darling Nell.

II.

She's ready to cry when I seem unkind,
But she smothers her grief within her mind ;
And when my spirit is soft and fond,
She sparkles the brightest of stars beyond.
Oh ! 'twould teach the thrushes to hear her sing,
And her sorrow the heart of a rock would wring ;
There never was saint but would leave his cell,
If he thought he could marry my Darling Nell !

LOVE CHANT.

I.

I THINK I've looked on eyes that shone
    With equal splendour,
And some, but they are dimmed and gone,
    As wildly tender.
I never looked on eyes that shed
    Such home-light mingled with such beauty—
That, 'mid all lights and shadows, said :
    "I love, and trust, and will be true to ye."

II.

I've seen some lips almost as red,
    A form as stately ;
And some such beauty turned my head
    Not very lately.
But not till now I've seen a girl
    With form so proud, lips so delicious,
With hair like night, and teeth of pearl--
    Who was not haughty and capricious.

III.

Oh, fairer than the dawn of day
    On Erne's islands !
Oh, purer than the thorn spray
    In Bantry's highlands !
In sleep such visions crossed my view,
    And when I woke the phantom faded ;
But now I find the fancy true,
    And fairer than the vision made it.

A CHRISTMAS SCENE:*

OR, LOVE IN THE COUNTRY.

I.

'THE hill blast comes howling through leaf-rifted
  trees,
'That late were as harp-strings to each gentle breeze;
'The strangers and cousins and every one flown,
'While we sit happy-hearted—together—alone.

II.

!Some are off to the mountains, and some to the fair,
'The snow is on their cheek, on mine your black hair;
Papa, with his farming, is busy to-day,
.And mamma's too good-natured to ramble this way.

III.

'The girls are gone—are they not?—into town,
'To fetch bows and bonnets, perchance a *beau* down.
.Ah! tell them, dear Kate, 'tis not fair to coquette—
.Though you, you bold lassie, are fond of it yet!

IV.

You're not—do you say?—just remember last night,
'You gave Harry a rose, and you dubbed him your
  knight:
!Poor lad! if he loved you—but no, darling! no,
'You're too thoughtful and good to fret any one so.

* See *Appendix* vi.

V.

The painters are raving of light and of shade,
And Harry, the poet, of lake, hill, and glade ;
While the light of your eye, and your soft wavy form
Suit a proser like me, by the hearth bright and warm.

VI.

The snow on those hills is uncommonly grand,
But, you know, Kate, it's not half so white as your
        hand ;
And say what you will of the grey Christmas sky,
Still I *slightly* prefer my dark girl's grey eye.

VII.

Be quiet, and sing me "The Bonny Cuckoo,"
For it bids us the summer and winter love through,
And then I'll read out an old ballad that shows
How Tyranny perished, and Liberty rose.

VIII.

My Kate ! I'm so happy, your voice whispers soft,
And your cheek flushes wilder from kissing so oft ;
For town or for country, for mountains or farms,
What care I ?—My darling's entwined in my arms.

THE INVOCATION.

AIR.—*Fanny Power.*

I.

Bright fairies by Glengariff's bay,
Soft woods that o'er Killarney sway,
Bold echoes born in Céim-an-eich,
      Your kinsman's greeting hear !
He asks you, by old friendship's name,
By all the rights that minstrels claim,
For Erin's joy and Desmond's fame,
      Be kind to Fanny dear !

II.

Her eyes are darker than Dunloe,
Her soul is whiter than the snow,
Her tresses like arbutus flow,
      Her step like frighted deer :
Then, still thy waves, capricious lake !
And ceaseless, soft winds, round her wake,
Yet never bring a cloud to break
      The smile of Fanny dear !

III.

Oh ! let her see the trance-bound men,
And kiss the red deer in his den,
And spy from out a hazel glen
      O'Donoghue appear ;—
Or, should she roam by wild Dunbwy,
Oh ! send the maiden to her knee,
Whilome I sung,—but then, ah ! me,
      I knew not Fanny dear !

IV.

Old Mangerton ! thine eagles plume—
Dear Innisfallen ! brighter bloom—
And Mucruss ! whisper thro' the gloom
        Quaint legends to her ear :
Till strong as ash-tree in its pride,
And gay as sunbeam on the tide,
We welcome back to Liffey's side,
        Our brightest, Fanny dear.

LOVE AND WAR.

I.

How soft is the moon on Glengariff !
    The rocks seem to melt with the light :
Oh ! would I were there with dear Fanny,
    To tell her that love is as bright ;
And nobly the sun of July
    O'er the waters of Adragoole shines—
Oh ! would that I saw the green banner
    Blaze there over conquering lines.

II.

Oh ! love is more fair than the moonlight,
    And glory more grand than the sun :
And there is no rest for a brave heart,
    Till its bride and its laurels are won ;
But next to the burst of our banner,
    And the smile of dear Fanny, I crave
The moon on the rocks of Glengariff—
    The sun upon Adragoole's wave.

MY LAND.

I.

She is a rich and rare land ;
Oh ! she's a fresh and fair land ;
She is a dear and rare land—
 This native land of mine.

II.

No men than her's are braver—
Her women's hearts ne'er waver ;
I'd freely die to save her,
 And think my lot divine.

III.

She's not a dull or cold land ;
No ! she's a warm and bold land ;
Oh ! she's a true and old land—
 This native land of mine.

IV.

Could beauty ever guard her,
And virtue still reward her,
No foe would cross her border—
 No friend within it pine !

V.

Oh ! she's a fresh and fair land ;
Oh ! she's a true and rare land ;
Yes ! she's a rare and fair land—
 This native land of mine.

THE RIGHT ROAD.

I.

Let the feeble-hearted pine,
Let the sickly spirit whine,
But work and win be thine,
    While you've life.
God smiles upon the bold—
So, when your flag's unrolled.
Bear it bravely till you're cold
    In the strife.

II.

If to rank or fame you soar,
Out your spirit frankly pour—
Men will serve you and adore,
    Like a king.
Woo your girl with honest pride,
Till you've won her for your bride—
Then to her, through time and tide,
    Ever cling.

III.

Never under wrongs despair ;
Labour long, and everywhere,
Link your countrymen, prepare,
    And strike home.
Thus have great men ever wrought,
Thus must greatness still be sought,
Thus laboured, loved, and fought
    Greece and Rome.

PART III.

HISTORICAL BALLADS AND SONGS.

First Series.

" THIS country of ours is no sand-bank, thrown up by some recent caprice of earth.   It is an ancient land, honoured in the archives of civilization, traceable into antiquity by its piety, its valour, and its sufferings.   Every great European race has sent its stream to the river of Irish mind.   Long wars, vast organisations, subtle codes, beacon crimes, leading virtues, and self-mighty men were here.   If we live influenced by wind, and sun, and tree, and not by the passions and deeds of the PAST, we are a thriftless and hopeless people."

DAVIS'S ESSAYS.

PART III.

BALLADS AND SONGS ILLUSTRATIVE OF IRISH HISTORY.

A NATION ONCE AGAIN.

I.

When boyhood's fire was in my blood,
    I read of ancient freemen,
For Greece and Rome who bravely stood,
    Three Hundred men and Three men.*
And then I prayed I yet might see
    Our fetters rent in twain,
And Ireland, long a province, be
    A Nation once again.

II.

And, from that time, through wildest woe,
    That hope has shone, a far light;
Nor could love's brightest summer glow
    Outshine that solemn starlight:

* The Three Hundred Greeks who died at Thermopylæ, and the Three Romans who kept the Sublician Bridge.

It seemed to watch above my head
    In forum, field, and fane ;
Its angel voice sang round my bed,
    "A Nation once again."

III.

It whispered, too, that "freedom's ark
    And service high and holy,
Would be profaned by feelings dark
    And passions vain or lowly :
For freedom comes from God's right hand,
    And needs a godly train ;
And righteous men must make our land
    A Nation once again."

IV.

So, as I grew from boy to man,
    I bent me to that bidding—
My spirit of each selfish plan
    And cruel passion ridding ;
For, thus I hoped some day to aid—·
    Oh ! can *such* hope be vain ?—
When my dear country shall be made
    A Nation once again.

LAMENT FOR THE MILESIANS.

Air—*An bruach na carraige báine.*

I.

Oh ! proud were the chieftains of green Inis-Fail ;
    *As truagh gan oidhir 'n-a bh-farradh !**
The stars of our sky, and the salt of our soil ;
    As truagh gan oidhir 'n-a bh-farradh !
Their hearts were as soft as a child in the lap,
Yet they were " the men in the gap "—
And now that the cold clay their limbs doth enwrap—
    As truagh gan oidhir 'n-a bh-farradh !

II.

'Gainst England long battling, at length they went
  down ;
    As truagh gan oidhir 'n-a bh-farradh !
But they left their deep tracks on the road of renown ;
    As truagh gan oidhir 'n-a bh-farradh !
We are heirs of their fame, if we're not of their race—
And deadly and deep our disgrace,
If we live o'er their sepulchres, abject and base ;—
    As truagh gan oidhir 'n-a bh-farradh !

III.

Oh ! sweet were the minstrels of kind Inis-Fail !
    As truagh gan oidhir 'n-a bh-farradh !
Whose music, nor ages, nor sorrow can spoil ;
    As truagh gan oidhir 'n-a bh-farradh !

---

* "That is a pity, without heir in their company," *i, e.* What a pity that there is no heir of their company. See the poem of Giolla Iosa Mor Mac Firbisigh in *The Genealogies, Tribes, and Customs of the Ui Fiachrach,* or *O'Dubhda's Country,* p. 230, line 2, and note d. Also *O'Reilly's Dict.* voce—*farradh.*

But their sad stifled tones are like streams flowing hid,
Their *caoine*** and their *piopracht*†† were chid,
And their language, "that melts into music," forbid;
  As truagh gan oidhir 'n-a bh-farradh !

IV.

How fair were the maidens of fair Inis-Fail !
  As truagh gan oidhir 'n-a bh-farradh !
As fresh and as free as the sea-breeze from soil;
  As truagh gan oidhir 'n-a bh-farradh !
Oh ! are not our maidens as fair and as pure ?
Can our music no longer allure ?
And can we but sob, as such wrongs we endure ?
  As truagh gan oidhir 'n-a bh-farradh !

V.

Their famous, their holy, their dear Inis-Fail !
  As truagh gan oidhir 'n-a bh-farradh !
Shall it still be a prey for the stranger to spoil ?
  As truagh gan oidhir 'n-a bh-farradh !
Sure, brave men would labour by night and by day
To banish that stranger away ;
Or, dying for Ireland, the future would say
  As truagh gan oidhir 'n-a bh-farradh !

VI.

Oh ! shame—for unchanged is the face of our isle ;
  As truagh gan oidhir 'n-a bh-farradh !
That taught them to battle, to sing, and to smile ;
  As truagh gan oidhir 'n-a bh-farradh !
We are heirs of their rivers, their sea, and their land,
Our sky and our mountains as grand—
We are heirs--oh, we're not--of their heart and their hand,
  As truagh gan oidhir 'n-a bh-farradh !

* *Anglice*, keen.   † *Angl.* pibroch.

THE FATE OF KING DATHI.

(A.D. 428.)*

I.

DARKLY their glibs o'erhang,
Sharp is their wolf-dog's fang.
Bronze spear and falchion clang—
    Brave men might shun them!
Heavy the spoil they bear—
Jewels and gold are there—
Hostage and maiden fair—
    How have they won them?

II.

From the soft sons of Gaul,
Roman, and Frank, and thrall,
Borough, and hut, and hall,—
    These have been torn.
Over Britannia wide,
Over fair Gaul they hied,
Often in battle tried,—
    Enemies mourn!

III.

Fiercely their harpers sing,—
Led by their gallant king,
They will to EIRE bring
    Beauty and treasure.
Britain shall bend the knee—
Rich shall their households be—
When their long ships the sea
    Homeward shall measure.

* *Vide* Appendix vii.

G

IV.

Parrow and Rath shall rise,
Towers. too, of wondrous size,
Táiltin they'll solemnize,
    Feis-Teamhrach assemble.
Samhain and Béal shall smile
On the rich holy isle—
Nay ! in a little while
    Œtius shall tremble.*

V.

Up on the glacier's snow,
Down on the vales below,
Monarch and clansmen go—
    Bright is the morning.
Never their march they slack,
Jura is at their back,
When falls the evening black,
    Hideous, and warning.

VI.

Eagles scream loud on high ;
Far off the chamois fly ;
Hoarse comes the torrent's cry,
    On the rocks whitening.
Strong are the storm's wings ;
Down the tall pine it flings ;
Hail-stone and sleet it brings—
    Thunder and lightning.

* The consul Œtius, the shield of Italy, and terror of " the barba-
rian," was a cotemporary of King Dathi. *Feis-Teamhrach*, the Parliament of Tara. *Táiltin*, games held at Taltte, county Meath. *Samhain*
and *Beal*, the moon and sun which Ireland worshipped.

VII.

Little these veterans mind
Thundering, hail, or wind ;
Closer their ranks they bind—
    Matching the storm.
While, a spear-cast or more,
On, the front ranks before,
DATHI the sunburst bore—
    Haughty his form.

VIII.

Forth from the thunder-cloud
Leaps out a foe as proud—
Sudden the monarch bowed—
    On rush the vanguard ;
Wildly the king they raise—
Struck by the lightning's blaze—
Ghastly his dying gaze,
    Clutching his standard !

IX.

Mild is the morning beam,
Gently the rivers stream,
Happy the valleys seem ;
    But the lone islanders—
Mark how they guard their king!
Hark, to the wail they sing !
Dark is their counselling—
    Helvetia's highlanders.

X.

Gather, like ravens, near—
Shall DATHI's soldiers fear ?
Soon their home-path they clear—
    Rapid and daring ;
On through the pass and plain,
Until the shore they gain,
And, with their spoil, again,
    Landed in EIRINN.

XI.

Little does EIRE* care
For gold or maiden fair—
" Where is King DATHI ?—where,
    Where is my bravest ?"
On the rich deck he lies,
O'er him his sunburst flies—
Solemn the obsequies,
    EIRE ! thou gavest.

XII.

See ye that countless train
Crossing Ros-Comain's† plain,
Crying, like hurricane,
    Uile liú ai ?
Broad is his *carn's* base—
Nigh the " King's burial-place,"‡
Last of the Pagan race,
    Lieth King DATHI !

---

* The true *ancient and modern* name of this island.
† *Angl.* Roscommon.
‡ *Hibernice*, Roilig na Riogh, *vulgo*, Relignaree—"A famous burial place near Cruachan, in Connacht, where the kings were usually interred, before the establishment of the Christian religion in Ireland."—
O'Brien's Ir. Dict.

ARGAN MÓR.*

Air.—*Argan Mor.*

I.

THE Danes rush around, around;
To the edge of the fosse they bound;
Hark! hark, to their trumpets' sound,
 Bidding them to the war.
Hark! hark to their cruel cry,
As they swear our hearts' cores to dry,
And their Raven red to dye;
 Glutting their demon, Thor.

II.

Leaping the Rath upon,
Here's the fiery Ceallachàn—
He makes the Lochlonnach† wan,
 Lifting his brazen spear!
Ivor, the Dane, is struck down,
For the spear broke right through his crown;
Yet worse did the battle frown—
 Anlaf is on our rere!

III.

See! see! the Rath's gates are broke!
And in—in, like a cloud of smoke,
Burst on the dark Danish folk,
 Charging us everywhere—
Oh, never was closer fight
Than in Argan Mór that night—
How.little do men want light,
 Fighting within their lair.

* *Vide* Appendix viii.   † Northmen

IV.

Then girding about our king,
On the thick of the foes we spring—
Down—down we trample and fling,
   Gallantly though they strive :
And never our falchions stood,
Till we were all wet with their blood,
And none of the pirate brood
   Went from the Rath alive !

THE VICTOR'S BURIAL.

I.

Wrap him in his banner, the best shroud of the brave—
Wrap him in his *onchu*,* and take him to his grave—
Lay him not down lowly, like bulwark overthrown,
But, gallantly upstanding, as if risen from his throne,
With his *craiseach*† in his hand, and his sword on his
  thigh,
With his war-belt on his waist, and his *cathbharr*‡ on
  high—
Put his *fleasg*§ upon his neck—his green flag round
  him fold,
Like ivy round a castle wall—not conquered, but
  grown old—
 '*Mhuire as truagh !   A mhuire as truagh !   A muhire
  as truagh !   ochon !*‖
 Weep for him !   Oh ! weep for him, but remember,
  in your moan,
 That he died, in his pride,—with his foes about him
  strown.

* Flag. † Spear. ‡ Helmet. § Collar. ‖ Wirrasthrue, ochone!

II.

Oh! shrine him in Beinn-Edair* with his face
    towards the foe,
As an emblem that not death our defiance can lay
    low—
Let him look across the waves from the promontory's
    breast,
To menace back the East, and to sentinel the West;
Sooner shall these channel waves the iron coast cut
    through,
Than the spirit he has left, yield, Easterlings! to
    you—
Let his coffin be the hill, let the eagles of the sea
Chorus with the surges round, the *tuircamh*† of the
    free!
    'Mhuire as truagh! A mhuire as truagh! A mhuire
    as truagh! ochon!
Weep for him! Oh! weep for him, but remember,
    in your moan,
That he died, in his pride—with his foes about
    him strown!

THE TRUE IRISH KING.‡

I.

The Cæsar of Rome has a wider domain,
And the *Ard Righ* of France has more clans in his
    train;
The sceptre of Spain is more heavy with gems,
And our crowns cannot vie with the Greek diadems;

---

* Howth.   † A masculine lament.   ‡ *Vide* Appendix ix.

But kinglier far before heaven and man
Are the Emerald fields, and the fiery-eyed clan,
The sceptre, and state, and the poets who sing,
And the swords that encircle A True Irish King !

II.

For, he must have come from a conquering race—
The heir of their valour, their glory, their grace :
His frame must be stately, his step must be fleet,
His hand must be trained to each warrior feat,
His face, as the harvest moon, steadfast and clear,
A head to enlighten, a spirit to cheer ;
While the foremost to rush where the battle-brands
    ring,
And the last to retreat, is A True Irish King !

III.

Yet, not for his courage, his strength, or his name,
Can he from the clansmen their fealty claim.
The poorest, and highest, choose freely to-day
The chief that, to-night, they'll as truly obey ;
For loyalty springs from a people's consent,
And the knee that is forced had been better unbent—
The Sacsanach serfs no such homage can bring
As the Irishmen's choice of A True Irish King !

IV.

Come, look on the pomp when they "make an
    O'Neill ;"
The muster of dynasts—O'h-Again, O'Shiadhail,
O'Catháin, O'h-Anluain,* O'Bhreisléin, and all,
From gentle Aird Uladh† to rude Dún na n-gall ;‡

* *Angl.* O'Hagan, O'Shiel, O'Cahan, or Kane, O'Hanlon.
† *Angl.* The Ards.   ‡ *Angl.* Donegal.

"St. Patrick's *comharba*,"* with bishops thirteen,
And *ollamhs*,† and *breitheamhs*,‡ and minstrels, are
  seen,
Round Tulach-Og§ Rath, like the bees in the spring,
All swarming to honour A TRUE IRISH KING !

V.

Unsandalled he stands on the foot-dinted rock,
Like a pillar-stone fixed against every shock.
Round, round is the Rath on a far-seeing hill,
Like his blemishless honour and vigilant will.
The grey-beards are telling how chiefs by the score
Have been crowned on "The Rath of the Kings"
  heretofore ;
While crowded, yet ordered, within its green ring,
Are the dynasts and priests round THE TRUE IRISH
  KING !

VI.

The chronicler read him the laws of the clan,
And pledged him to bide by their blessing and ban ;
His *skian* and his sword are unbuckled to show
That they only were meant for a foreigner foe ;
A white willow wand has been put in his hand—
A type of pure, upright, and gentle command—
While hierarchs are blessing, the slipper they fling,
And O'Catháin proclaims him A TRUE IRISH KING !

---

* Successor—*comharba Phadruig*—the Archbishop of *Ard-macha*
(Armagh).
† Doctors or learned men.   ‡ Judges. *Angl.* Brehons
§ In the county *Tir-Eoghain* (Tyrone) between Cookstown and
Stewartstown.

VII.

Thrice looked he to Heaven with thanks and with
　　prayer—
Thrice looked to his borders with sentinel stare—
To the waves of Loch n-Eathach,* the heights of
　　Srathbhán ;†
And thrice on his allies, and thrice on his clan—
One clash on their bucklers !—one more !—they are
　　still—
What means the deep pause on the crest of the hill?
Why gaze they above him ?—a war-eagle's wing !
"'Tis an omen !—Hurrah! for THE TRUE IRISH
　　KING !"

VIII.

God aid him !—God save him !—and smile on his
　　reign—
The terror of England—the ally of Spain.
May his sword be triumphant o'er Sacsanach arts !
Be his throne ever girt by strong hands and true
　　hearts !
May the course of his conquest run on till he see
The flag of Plantagenet sink in the sea !
May minstrels for ever his victories sing,
And saints make the bed of THE TRUE IRISH KING !

* *Angl.* Lough Neagh.　　　　　　† *Angl.* Strabane.

THE GERALDINES.

I.

The Geraldines ! the Geraldines !—tis full a thousand
years
Since, 'mid the Tuscan vineyards, bright flashed their
battle-spears ;
When Capet seized the crown of France, their iron
shields were known,
And their sabre-dint struck terror on the banks of the
Garonne :
Across the downs of Hastings they spurred hard by
William's side,
And the grey sands of Palestine with Moslem blood
they dyed ;
But never then, nor thence, till now, has falsehood
or disgrace
Been seen to soil Fitzgerald's plume, or mantle in his
face.

II.

The Geraldines ! the Geraldines !—'tis true, in Strongbow's van,
By lawless force, as conquerors, their Irish reign
began ;
And, oh ! through many a dark campaign they proved
their prowess stern,
In Leinster's plains, and Munster's vales, on king, and
chief, and kerne ;
But noble was the cheer within the halls so rudely
won,
And generous was the steel-gloved hand that had such
slaughter done ;

How gay their laugh, how proud their mien, you'd ask
no herald's sign—
Among a thousand you had known the princely Geraldine.

III.

These Geraldines! these Geraldines!—not long our
air they breathed;
Not long they fed on venison, in Irish water seethed;
Not often had their children been by Irish mothers
nursed;
When from their full and genial hearts an Irish feel-
ing burst!
The English monarchs strove in vain, by law, and
force, and bribe,
To win from Irish thoughts and ways this " more than
Irish" tribe;
For still they clung to fosterage, to *breitheamh*, cloak,
and bard:
What king dare say to Geraldine, "your Irish wife
discard?"

IV.

Ye Geraldines! ye Geraldines!—how royally ye
reigned
O'er Desmond broad, and rich Kildare, and English
arts disdained:
Your sword made knights, your banner waved, free
was your bugle call
By Gleann's* green slopes, and Daingean's† tide, from
Bearbha's‡ banks to Eóchaill.§

* *Angl.* Glyn.
‡ *Angl.* Barrow.
† *Angl.* Dingle.
§ *Angl.* Youghal.

What gorgeous shrines, what *breitheamh** lore, what
    minstrel feasts there were
In and around Magh Nuadhaid's† keep, and palace-
    filled Adare !
But not for rite or feast ye stayed, when friend or kin
    were pressed ;
And foemen fled, when *" Crom Abú"*‡ bespoke your
    lance in rest.

V.

Ye Geraldines ! ye Geraldines !—since Silken Thomas
    flung
King Henry's sword on council board, the English
    thanes among,
Ye never ceased to battle brave against the English
    sway,
Though axe, and brand, and treachery, your proudest
    cut away.
Of Desmond's blood, through woman's veins passed
    on th' exhausted tide ;
His title lives—a Sacsanach churl usurps the lion's
    hide ;
And, though Kildare tower haughtily, there's ruin at
    the root,
Else why, since Edward fell to earth, had such a tree
    no fruit ?

VI.

True Geraldines ! brave Geraldines !—as torrents
    mould the earth,
You channelled deep old Ireland's heart by constancy
    and worth :

* *Angl.* Brehon.	† *Angl.* Maynooth.
‡ Formerly the war-cry of the Geraldines, and now their motto.

When Ginckle 'leaguered Limerick, the Irish soldiers
    gazed
To see if in the setting sun dead Desmond's banner
    blazed ?
And still it is the peasants' hope upon the Cuirreach's*
    mere,
" They live, who'll see ten thousand men with good
    Lord Edward here "—
So let them dream till brighter days, when, not by
    Edward's shade,
But by some leader true as he, their lines shall be
    arrayed !

VII.

These Geraldines ! these Geraldines ;—rain wears
    away the rock,
And time may wear away the tribe that stood the
    battle's shock ;
But ever, sure, while one is left of all that honoured
    race,
In front of Ireland's chivalry is that Fitzgerald's
    place :
And, though the last were dead and gone, how many
    a field and town,
From Thomas Court to Abbeyfeile, would cherish
    their renown,
And men would say of valour's rise, or ancient power's
    decline,
" Twill never soar, it never shone, as did the Ger-
    aldine,"

* *Angl.* Curragh.

VIII.

The Geraldines ! the Geraldines !—and are there any
    fears
Within the sons of conquerors for full a thousand years?
Can treason spring from out a soil bedewed with
    martyr's blood ?
Or has that grown a purling brook, which long rushed
    down a flood ?—
By Desmond swept with sword and fire,—by clan and
    keep laid low,—
By silken Thomas and his kin,—by sainted Edward, no !
The forms of centuries rise up, and in the Irish line
COMMAND THEIR SON TO TAKE THE POST THAT FITS
    THE GERALDINE !*

O'BRIEN OF ARA.†

AIR.—*The Piper of Blessington.*

I.

TALL are the towers of O'Ceinneidigh.—‡
    Broad are the lands of MacCarrthaigh—§
Desmond feeds five hundred men a-day ;
    Yet, here's to O'Briain‖ of Ara !
        Up from the Castle of Druim-aniar,¶
        Down from the top of Camailte,
        Clansman and kinsman are coming here
        To give him the CEAD MILE FAILTE.

* The concluding stanza was found among the author's papers, and
was inserted in the first edition. The allusion to the pure, honest,
W. Smith O'Brien, is obvious.

† Ara is a small mountain tract, south of Loch Deirgdheire, and north
of the Camailte, or the Keeper, hills. It was the seat of a branch of
of the Thomond princes, called the O'Briens of Ara.

‡ *Vulgo.* O'Kennedy.   § *Vul.* M'Carthy.
‖ *Vul.* O'Brien.   ¶ *Vul.* Drumineer.

II.

See you the mountains look huge at eve—
  So is our chieftain in battle—
Welcome he has for the fugitive,—
  *Uisce-beatha** fighting, and cattle !
Up from the Castle of Druim-aniar,
  Down from the top of Camailte,
Gossip and ally are coming here
  To give him the CEAD MILE FAILTE.

III.

Horses the valleys are tramping on,
  Sleek from the Sacsanach manger—
Creachs the hills are encamping on,
  Empty the bâns of the stranger !
    Up from the Castle of Druim-aniar,
      Down from the top of Camailte,
    Ceithearn† and *buannacht* are coming here
      To give him the CEAD MILE FAILTE.

IV.

He has black silver from Cill-da-lua—‡
  Rian§ and Cearbhall‖ are neighbours—
'N Aonach¶ submits with a *fuilliú*—
  Butler is meat for our sabres !
    Up from the Castle of Druim-aniar,
      Down from the top of Camailte,
    Rian and Cearbhall are coming here
      To give him the CEAD MILE FAILTE.

---

* *Vul.* Usquebaugh.   † *Vulgo,* Kerne.   ‡ *Vul.* Killaloe.
§ *Vul.* Ryan.   ‖ *Vul.* Carroll.   ¶ *Vul.* Nenagh.

V.

'Tis scarce a week since through Osairghe*
   Chased he the Baron of Durmhagh—†
Forced him five rivers to cross, or he
   Had died by the sword of Red Murchadh !‡
      Up from the Castle of Drum-aniar,
      Down from the top of Camailte,
    All the Ui Bhriain are coming here
      To give him the CEAD MILE FAILTE.

VI.

Tall are towers of O'Ceinneidigh—
   Broad are the lands of MacCarrthaigh—
Desmond feeds five hundred men a-day ;
   Yet, here's to O'Briain of Ara !
      Up from the Castle of Druim-aniar,
      Down from the top of Camailte,
    Clansman and kinsman are coming here
      To give him the CEAD MILE FAILTE.

* *Vulgo*, Ossory.   † *Vul.* Durrow.   ‡ *Vul.* Murrough.

EMMELINE TALBOT.

A BALLAD OF THE PALE.

[The scene is on the borders of Dublin and Wicklow.]

I.

'Twas a September day,
　　In Glenismole,*
Emmeline Talbot lay
　　On a green knoll.
She was a lovely thing,
Fleet as a falcon's wing,
Only fifteen that spring—
　　Soft was her soul.

II.

Danger and dreamless sleep
　　Much did she scorn,
And from her father's keep
　　Stole out that morn.
Towards Glenismole she hies—
Sweetly the valley lies,
Winning the enterprise—
　　No one to warn.

III.

Till, by the noon, at length,
　　High in the vale,
Emmeline found her strength
　　Suddenly fail.

---

* *Hibernice*, Gleann-an-smóil.

Panting, yet pleasantly,
By Dodder-side lay she—
Thrushes sang merrily,
  "Hail, sister, hail!"

IV.

Hazel and copse of oak
  Made a sweet lawn,
Out from the thicket broke
  Rabbit and fawn.
Green were the *eiscirs* round,
Sweet was the river's sound,
Eastwards flat Cruach frowned,
  South lay Sliabh Bân.

V.

Looking round Barnakeel,*
  Like a tall Moor
Full of impassioned zeal
  Peeped brown Kippure.†
Dublin in feudal pride
And many a hold beside,
Over Finn-ghaill‡ preside—
  Sentinels sure!

VI.

Is that a roebuck's eye
  Glares from the green?—
Is that a thrush's cry
  Rings in the screen?

---

* *Hib.* Bearna-chael.   † *Hib.* Keap-lúbhair.   ‡ *Vulg.* Fingal.

Mountaineers round her sprung,
Savage their speech and tongue
Fierce was their chief, and young,
    Poor Emmeline !

VII.

" Hurrah, 'tis Talbot's child,"
    Shouted the kerne,
" Off to the mountains wild,
    Faire,* O'Byrne !"
Like a bird in a net,
Strove the sweet maiden yet,
Praying and shrieking, " Let—
    Let me return."

VIII.

After a moment's doubt,
    Forward he sprung,
With his sword flashing out—
    Wrath on his tongue.
" Touch not a hair of her's—
Dies he, who finger stirs !"
Back fell his foragers,
    To him she clung.

IX.

Soothing the maiden'a fears,
    Kneeling was he,
When burst old Talbot's spears
    Out on the lea.

* *Vulg.* Farrah.

March-men, all stanch and stout
Shouting their Belgard shout—
" Down with the Irish rout,
    " *Prets d'accomplir.*"*

X.

Taken thus unawares,
    Some fled amain ;
Fighting like forest bears,
    Others were slain.
To the chief clung the maid,
How could he use his blade ?
That night, upon him weighed
    Fetter and chain.

XI.

Oh ! but that night was long,
    Lying forlorn,
Since, 'mid the wassail song,
    These words were borne—
" Nathless your tears and cries,
Sure as the sun shall rise,
Connor O'Byrne† dies,
    Talbot has sworn."

XII.

Brightly on Tamlacht‡ hill
    Flashes the sun,
Strained at his window-sill,
    How his eyes run

* The motto and cry of the Talbots.   † *Hib.* Conchobhar O'Broin.
    ‡ *Vulg.* Tallaght.

From lonely Sagart slade
Down to Tigh-bradán glade,
Landmarks of border raid,
  Many a one.

XIII.

Too well the captive knows
  Belgard's main wall
Will, to his naked blows,
  Shiver and fall,
Ere in his mountain hold
He shall again behold
Those whose proud hearts are cold,
  Weeping his thrall.

XIV.

" Oh ! for a mountain side,
  Bucklers and brands !
Freely I could have died
  Heading my bands,
But on a felon tree—"
Bearing a fetter-key,
By him all silently,
  Emmeline stands.

XV.

Last rose the castellan,
  He had drunk deep,—
Warder and serving-man
  Still were asleep,—
Wide is the castle-gate,
Open the captive's grate,
Fetters disconsolate
  Flung in a heap.   *   *

XVI.

'Tis an October day,
  Close by Loch Dan
Many a *creach* lay,
  Many a man.
'Mongst them, in gallant mien,
Connor O'Byrne's seen
Wedded to Emmeline,
  Girt by his clan!

O'SULLIVAN'S RETURN. *

AIR—*An cruisgin lán.*

O'SUILLEBHAIN has come
Within sight of his home,—
  He had left it long years ago ;
The tears are in his eyes,
And he prays the wind to rise,
As he looks towards his castle, from the prow, from
  the prow ;
As he looks towards his castle, from the prow.

II.

For the day had been calm,
And slow the good ship swam,
  And the evening gun had been fired ;
He knew the hearts beat wild
Of mother, wife, and child,
And of clans, who to see him long desired, long de-
  sired ;
And of clans, who to see him long desired.

* *Vide* Appendix x.

III.

Of the tender ones the clasp,
Of the gallant ones the grasp,
　　He thinks, until his tears fall warm ;
And full seems his wide hall,
With friends from wall to wall,
Where their welcome shakes the banners, like a storm.
　　like a storm ;
Where their welcome shakes the banners like a storm.

IV.

Then he sees another scene—
Normal churls on the green—
　　" *O'Suilleabháin abú* " is the cry ;
For filled is his ship's hold
With arms and Spanish gold,
And he sees the snake-twined spear wave on high,
　　wave on high ;
And he sees the snake-twined spear wave on high.*

V.

" Finghin's race shall be freed—
From the Norman's cruel breed—
My sires freed Béar once before,

---

* The standard bearings of O'Sullivan. See O'Donovan's edition of
the Banquet of Dún na n-Gedh, and the Battle of Magh Rath, for the
Archæological Society, App. p. 349.—"Bearings of O'Sullivan at the
Battle of Caisglinn."

　" I see, mightily advancing on the plain,
　　The banner of the race of noble Finghin ;
　　His spear with a venemous adder (*entwined*),
　　His host all fiery champions."
Finghin was one of their most famous progenitors.—AUTHOR'S NOTE.

When the Barnwell's were strewn
On the fields, like hay in June,
And but one of them escaped from our shore, from
    our shore ;
And but one of them escaped from our shore."*

VI.

And, warming in his dream,
He floats on victory's stream,
    Till Desmond—till all Erin is free !
Then, how calmly he'll go down,
Full of years and of renown,
To his grave near that castle by the sea, by the sea ;
To his grave near that castle by the sea !

VII.

But the wind heard his word,
As though he were its lord,
    And the ship is dashed up the Bay.
Alas ! for that proud barque,
The night has fallen dark,
'Tis too late to Eadarghabhal† to bear away, to bear
    away ;
'Tis too late to Eadarghabail to bear away.

VIII.

Black and rough was the rock,
And terrible the shock,
    As the good ship crashed asunder ;

* The Barnwells were Normans, who seized part of Beara in the reign
of Henry II.; but the O'Sullivan's came down on them, and cut off all
save one—a young man who settled at Drimnagh Castle, Co. Dublin,
and was ancestor to the Barnwells, Lords of Trimlestone and Kingsland.
—AUTHOR'S NOTE.
    † *Vul.* Adragoole.

Aud bitter was the cry,
Aud the sea ran mountains high,
And the wind was as loud as the thunder, the thunder,
And the wind was as loud as the thunder.

IX.

There's woe in Béara,
There's woe in Gleann-garbh,*
   And from Beánntráighe† unto Dùn-
     kiaráin ;‡
All Desmond hears their grief,
And wails above their chief—
"Is it thus, is it thus, that you return, you return—
Is it thus, is it thus, that you return?"

THE FATE OF THE O'SULLIVANS.§

I.

"A BABY in the mountain gap—
  Oh! wherefore bring it hither?
Restore it to it's mother's lap,
  Or else 'twill surely wither.

* *Vul.* Glengariff.   † *Vul.* Bantry.   ‡ *Vul.* Dunkerron.

§ After the taking of Dunbwy and the ruin of the O'Sullivan's country, the chief marched right through Muskerry and Ormond, hotly pursued. He crossed the Shannon in *curachs* made of his horses' skins. He then defeated the English forces and slew their commander, Manby, and finally fought his way into O'Ruare's country. During his absence his lady (*Beantighearna*) and infant were supported in the mountains, by one of his clansmen, M'Swiney, who, tradition says, used to rob the eagles' nests of their prey for his charge. O'Sullivan was excepted from James the First's amnesty on account of his persevering resistance. He went to Spain, and was appointed governor of Corunna and Viscount Berehaven. His march from Glengariff to Leitrim is, perhaps, the most romantic and gallant achievement of his age.—AUTHOR'S NOTE.

A baby near the eagle's nest !
   How should their talons spare it ?
Oh ! take it to some woman's breast,
   And she will kindly care it."

II.

" Fear not for it," M'Swiney said,
   And stroked his *cul-fionn** slowly,
And proudly raised his matted head,
   Yet spoke me soft and lowly—
" Fear not for it, for, many a day,
   I climb the eagle's eyrie,
And bear the eaglet's food away
   To feed our little fairy.

III.

" Fear not for it, no Bantry bird
   Would harm our chieftain's baby"—
He stopped, and something in him stirred—
   'Twas for his chieftain, maybe.
And then he brushed his softened eyes,
   And raised his bonnet duly,
And muttered "the *Beantigherna* lies
   Asleep in yonder *buaili*."†

IV.

He pointed 'twixt the cliff and lake,
   And there a hut of heather,
Half hidden in the craggy brake,
   Gave shelter from the weather ;

---

* *Vulgo*, coulin.   † *Vulgo*, boulie.

The little tanist shrieked with joy,
　　Adown the gulley staring—
The clansman swelled to see the boy,
　　O'Sullivan-like, daring.

V.

Oh! what a glorious sight was there,
　　As from the summit gazing,
O'er winding creek and islet fair,
　　And mountain waste amazing;
The Caha and Dunkerron hills
　　Cast half the gulfs in shadow,
While shone the sun on Guliagh's rills,
　　And Whiddy's emerald meadow—

VI.

The sea a sheet of crimson spread,
　　From Foze to Dursey islands;
While flashed the peaks from Mizenhead
　　To Musk'ry's distant highlands—
I saw no kine, I saw no sheep,
　　I saw nor house nor furrow;
But round the tarns the red deer leap,
　　Oak and arbutus thorough.

VII.

Oh! what a glorious sight was there,
　　That paradise o'ergazing—
When, sudden, burst a smoky glare,
　　Above Glengariff blazing—
The clansman sprung upon his feet—
　　Well might the infant wonder—
His hands were clenched, his brow was knit,
　　His hard lips just asunder.

VIII.

Like shattered rock from out the ground,
    He stood there stiff and silent—
Our breathing hardly made a sound,
    As o'er the baby I leant ;
His figure then went to and fro,
    As the tall blaze would flicker—
And as exhausted it sunk low,
    His breath came loud and thicker.

IX.

Then slowly turned he round his head,
    And slowly turned his figure ;
His eye was fixed as Spanish lead,
    His limbs were full of rigour—
Then suddenly he grasped the child,
    And raised it to his shoulder,
Then pointing where, across the wild,
    The fire was seen to smoulder.

X.

" Look, baby !—look, there is the sign,
    Your father is returning,
The 'generous hand' of Finghin's line
    Has set that beacon burning.
' The generous hand'—Oh ! Lord of hosts—
    Oh, Virgin, ever holy !
There's nought to give on Bantry's coasts—
    Dunbwy* is lying lowly.

* *Vide* Appendix xi.

XI.

" The halls, where mirth and minstrelsy
  Than Béara's wind rose louder,
Are flung in masses lonelily,
  And black with English powder—
The sheep that o'er our mountains ran,
  The kine that filled our valleys,
Are gone, and not a single clan
  O'Sullivan now rallies.

XII.

" He, long the Prince of hill and bay !
  The ally of the Spaniard !
Has scarce a single *cath* to-day,
  Nor seaman left to man yard "—
M'Swiney ceased, then fiercely strode,
  Bearing along the baby,
Until we reached the rude abode
  Of Bantry's lovely lady.

XIII.

We found her in the savage shed—
  ,A mild night in midwinter—
The mountain heath her only bed,
  Her dais the rocky splinter !
The sad *Beantigliearn'* had seen the fire—
  'Twas plain she had been praying—
She seized her son, as we came nigher,
  And welcomed me, thus saying—

XIV.

" Our gossip's friend I gladly greet,
　　Though scant'ly I can cheer him ;"
Then bids the clansmen fly to meet
　　And tell her lord she's near him.
M'Swiney kissed his foster son,
　　And shouting out his *faire*
" *O' Suillebháin abú*"—is gone
　　Like Marchman's deadly arrow !

XV.

An hour went by, when, from the shore
　　The chieftain's horn winding,
Awoke the echoes' hearty roar—
　　Their fealty reminding :
A moment, and he faintly gasps—
　　" These—these, thank heav'n, are left me "—
And smiles, as wife and child he clasps—
　　" They have not quite bereft me."

XVI.

I never saw a mien so grand,
　　A brow and eye so fearless—
There was not in his veteran band
　　A single eyelid tearless.
His tale is short—O'Ruarc's strength
　　Could not postpone his ruin,
And Leitrim's towers he left at length,
　　To spare his friend's undoing.

XVII.

To Spain—to Spain, he now will sail,
　　His destiny is wroken—
An exile from dear Inis-fail,—
　　Nor yet his will is broken ;
For still he hints some enterprise,
　　When fleets shall bring them over,
Dunbwy's proud keep again shall rise,
　　And mock the English rover.　*　*　*

XVIII.

I saw them cross Slieve Miskisk o'er,
　　The crones around them weeping—
I saw them pass from Culiagh's shore,
　　Their galleys' strong oars sweeping ;
I saw their ship unfurl its sail—
　　I saw their scarfs long waven—
They saw the hills in distance fail—
　　They never saw Berehaven !

THE SACK OF BALTIMORE.*

I.

THE summer sun is falling soft on Carbery's hundred
isles—
The summer sun is gleaming still through Gabriel's
rough defiles—
Old Inisherkin's crumbled fane looks like a moulting
bird ;
And in a calm and sleepy swell the ocean tide is
heard ;
The hookers lie upon the beach ; the children cease
their play ;
The gossips leave the little inn ; the households kneel
to pray—
And full of love, and peace, and rest—its daily labour
o'er—
Upon that cosy creek there lay the town of Baltimore.

II.

A deeper rest, a starry trance, has come with midnight
there ;
No sound, except that throbbing wave, in earth, or
sea, or air.

* Baltimore is a small seaport in the barony of Curbery, in South
Munster. It grew up round a Castle of O'Driscoll's, and was, after his
ruin, colonized by the English: On the 20th of June, 1631, the crew of
two Algerine galleys landed in the dead of the night, sacked the town,
and bore off into slavery all who were not too old, or too young, or too
fierce for their purpose. The pirates were steered up the intricate
channel by one Hackett, a Dungarvan fisherman, whom they had taken
at sea for the purpose. Two years after he was convicted and executed
for the crime. Baltimore never recovered this. To the artist, tho
antiquary, and the naturalist, its neighbourhood is most interesting.—
See "The Ancient and Present State of the County and City of Cork,"
by Charles Smith, M. D.

The massive capes, and ruined towers, seem conscious
     of the calm ;
The fibrous sod and stunted trees are breathing heavy
     balm.
So still the night, these two long barques, round
     Dunashad that glide,
Must trust their oars—methinks not few—against the
     ebbing tide—
Oh ! some sweet mission of true love must urge them
     to the shore—
They bring some lover to his bride, who sighs in
     Baltimore !

III.

All, all asleep within each roof along that rocky street,
And these must be the lover's friends, with gently
     gliding feet—
A stifled gasp ! a dreamy noise ! "the roof is in a
     flame !"
From out their beds, and to their doors, rush maid,
     and sire, and dame—
And meet, upon the threshold stone, the gleaming
     sabre's fall,
And o'er each black and bearded face the white or
     crimson shawl—
The yell of " Allah " breaks above the prayer, and
     shriek and roar—
Oh, blessed God ! the Algerine is lord of Baltimore !

IV.

Then flung the youth his naked hand against the
     shearing sword ;
Then sprung the mother on the brand with which her
     son was gored ;

Then sunk the grandsire on the floor, his grand-babes
    clutching wild ;
Then fled the maiden moaning faint, and nestled with
    the child ;
But see, yon pirate strangled lies, and crushed with
    splashing heel,
While o'er him in an Irish hand there sweeps his
    Syrian steel—
Though virtue sink, and courage fail, and misers yield
    their store,
There's *one* hearth well avengéd in the sack of Balti-
    more !

v.

Mid-summer morn, in woodland nigh, the birds began
    to sing—
They see not now the milking maids—deserted is the
    spring !
Mid-summer day—this gallant rides from distant
    Bandon's town—
These hookers crossed from stormy Skull, that skiff
    from Affadown ;
They only found the smoking walls, with neighbours'
    blood besprent,
And on the strewed and trampled beach awhile they
    wildly went—
Then dashed to sea, and passed Cape Cléire, and saw
    five leagues before
The pirate galleys vanishing that ravaged Baltimore.

VI.

Oh ! some must tug the galley's oar, and some must
    tend the steed—
This boy will bear a Scheik's chibouk, and that a Bey's
    jerreed.

Oh ! some are for the arsenals, by beauteous Dardan-
    elles ;
And some are in the caravan to Mecca's sandy dells.
The maid that Bandon gallant sought is chosen for
    the Dey—
She's safe—he's dead—she stabbed him in the midst
    of his Serai ;
And, when to die a death of fire, that noble maid they
    bore,
She only smiled—O'Driscoll's child—she thought of
    Baltimore.

VII.

'Tis two long years since sunk the town beneath
    that bloody band,
And all around its trampled hearths a larger concourse
    stand,
Where, high upon a gallows tree, a yelling wretch is
    seen—
'Tis Hackett of Dungarvan—he, who steered the
    Algerine !
He fell amid a sullen shout, with scarce a passing
    prayer,
For he had slain the kith and kin of many a hundred
    there--
Some muttered of MacMurchadh, who brought the
    Norman o'er—
Some cursed him with Iscariot, that day in Baltimore.

LAMENT FOR THE DEATH OF EOGHAN RUADH O'NEILL.*

₊ Time, 10th Nov. 1649. Scene—Ormond's Camp, County Waterford. Speakers—A veteran of Eoghan O'Neill's clan, and one of the horsemen, just arrived with an account of his death.

I.

" Did they dare, did they dare, to slay Eoghan Ruadh
    O'Neill ?"
" Yes, they slew with poison him, they feared to meet
    with steel."
" May God wither up their hearts ! May their blood
    cease to flow !
" May they walk in living death, who poisoned Eoghan
    Ruadh !

II.

" Though it break my heart to hear, say again the bitter
    words."
" From Derry, against Cromwell, he marched to mea-
    sure swords :
But the weapon of the Sacsanach met him on his way,
And he died at Cloch Uachtar,† upon St. Leonard's
    day.

III.

" Wail, wail ye for the Mighty One ! Wail, wail, ye
    for the Dead !
' Quench the hearth, and hold the breath—with ashes
    strew the head.

---

* Commonly called Owen Roe O'Neill. *Vide* Appendix xii.
† Clough Oughter.

How tenderly we loved him ! How deeply we deplore !
Holy Saviour ! but to think we shall never see him
more.

IV.

" Sagest in the council was he, kindest in the hall !
Sure we never won a battle—'twas Eoghan won them
all.
Had he lived—had he lived —our dear country had
been free ;
But he's dead, but he's dead, and 'tis slaves we'll ever
be.

V.

"O'Farrell and Clanrickarde, Preston and Red Hugh,
Audley, and MacMahon, ye are valiant, wise, and
true ;
But—what, what are ye all to our darling who is
gone ?
The Rudder of our Ship was he, our Castle's corner
stone !

VI.

" Wail, wail him through the Island ! Weep, weep, for
our pride !
Would that on the battle-field our gallant chief had
died !
Weep the Victor of Beann-bhorbh*—weep him, young
men and old ;
Weep for him, ye women—your Beautiful lies cold !

* Benburb.

VII.

"We thought you would not die—we were sure you
 would not go,
And leave us in our utmost need to Cromwell's cruel
 blow—
Sheep without a shepherd, when the snow shuts out
 the sky—
Oh! why did you leave us, Eoghan? Why did you
 die?

VIII.

"Soft as woman's was your voice, O'Neill! bright was
 your eye,
Oh! why did you leave us, Eoghan? Why did you
 die?
Your troubles are all over, you're at rest with God on
 high,
But we're slaves, and we're orphans, Eoghan!—why
 didst thou die?"

A RALLY FOR IRELAND.

May, 1689.*

I.

Shout it out, till it ring,
 From Beann-mhór to Cape Cléire,
For our country and king,
 And religion so dear.

* *Vide* Appendix xiii.

Rally, men ! rally—
Irishmen ! rally !
Gather round the dear flag, that, wet with our tears,
And torn, and bloody, lay hid for long years,
And now, once again, in its pride re-appears.
See ! from the Castle our green banner waves,
Bearing fit motto for uprising slaves—
For Now or Never !
Now and for ever !
Bids you to battle for triumph or graves—
Bids you to burst on the Sacsanach knaves—
Rally, then, rally !
Irishmen, rally !
Shout Now or never !
Now and for ever !
Heed not their fury, however it raves,
Welcome their horsemen with pikes and with
staves,
Close on their cannon, their bay'nets, and glaives,
Down with their standard wherever it waves ;
Fight to the last, and ye cannot be slaves !
Fight to the last, and ye cannot be slaves !

II.

Gallant Sheldon is here,
And Hamilton, too,
And Tirchonaill so dear,
And MacCarrthaigh, so true.
And there are Frenchmen ;
Skilful and stanch men —
De Rosen, Pontée, Pusignan, and Boisseleau,
And gallant Lauzun is a coming, you know,
With Balldearg, the kinsman of great Eoghan Ruadh.

From Sionainn to Banna, from Lifé to Laoi,*
The country is rising for Libertie.
    Tho' your arms are rude,
    If your courage be good,
As the traitor fled will the stranger flee,
At another Drom-mór from the " Irishry."
    Arm, peasant and lord !
    Grasp musket and sword !
    Grasp pike-staff and *skian* !
    Give your horses the rein !
March, in the name of his Majesty—
Ulster and Munster unitedly—
Townsman and peasant, like waves of the sea—
Leinster and Connacht to victory—
Shoulder to shoulder for Liberty,
Shoulder to shoulder for Liberty.

III.

    Kirk, Schomberg and Churchill
    Are coming—what then ?
We'll drive them and Dutch Will
    To England again ;
    We can laugh at each threat.
    For our Parliament's met—
De Courcy, O'Brian, Mac Domhaill, Le Poer,
O'Neill and St. Lawrence, and others *go leor*,
The choice of the land from Athluain† to the shore !
They'll break the last link of the Sacsanach chain !
They'll give us the lands of our fathers again !

---

  * Shannon, Bann, Liffey, and Lee.   † Athlone.

Then up ye ! and fight
For your King and your Right,
Or ever toil on, and never complain
Tho' they trample your roof-tree, and rifle your fane.
Rally, then, rally !
Irishmen, rally—
Fight Now or never,
Now and for ever !
Laws are in vain without swords to maintain ;
So, muster as fast as the fall of the rain :
Serried and rough as a field of ripe grain,
Stand by your flag upon mountain and plain :
Charge till yourselves or your foemen are slain !
Fight till yourselves or your foemen are slain !

THE BATTLE OF LIMERICK.*

August 27, 1690.

Air—*Garradh Eoghain.*†

I.

Oh, hurrah ! for the men who, when danger is nigh,
Are found in the front, looking death in the eye.
Hurrah ! for the men who kept Limerick's wall,
And hurrah ! for bold Sarsfield, the bravest of all.
King William's men round Limerick lay,
His cannon crashed from day to day,
Till the southern wall was swept away
At the city of *Luimneach linn-ghlas.*‡

---

* *Vide* Appendix xlv.   † Garryowen.
‡ "Limerick of the azure river."

'Tis afternoon, yet hot the sun,
When William fires the signal gun,
And, like its flash, his columns run
    On the city of *Luimneach linn-ghlas.*

II.

Yet, hurrah! for the men who, when danger is nigh,
Are found in the front, looking death in the eye.
Hurrah! for the men who kept Limerick's wall,
And hurrah! for bold Sarsfield, the bravest of all.
    The breach gaped out two perches wide,
    The fosse is filled, the batteries plied;
    Can the Irishmen that onset bide
        At the city of *Luimneach linn-ghlas.*
Across the ditch the columns dash,
Their bayonets o'er the rubbish flash,
When sudden comes a rending crash
    From the city of *Luimneach linn-ghlas.*

III.

Then, hurrah! for the men who, when danger is nigh,
Are found in the front, looking death in the eye.
Hurrah! for the men who kept Limerick's wall,
And hurrah! for bold Sarsfield, the bravest of all.
    The bullets rain in pelting shower,
    And rocks and beams from wall and tower;
    The Englishmen are glad to cower
        At the city of *Luimneach linn-ghlas.*
But, rallied soon, again they pressed,
Their bayonets pierced full many a breast,
Till they bravely won the breach's crest
    At the city of *Luimneach linn-ghlas.*

IV.

Yet, hurrah ! for the men who, when danger is nigh,
Are found in the front, looking death in the eye.
Hurrah ! for the men who kept Limerick's wall,
And hurrah ! for bold Sarsfield, the bravest of all.
 Then fiercer grew the Irish yell,
 And madly on the foe they fell,
 Till the breach grew like the jaws of hell—
  Not the city of *Luimneach linn-ghlas.*
 The women fought before the men,
 Each man became a match for ten,
 So back they pushed the villains then,
  From the city of *Luimneach linn-ghlas.*

V.

Then, hurrah ! for the men who, when danger is nigh,
Are found in the front, looking death in the eye.
Hurrah ! for the men who kept Limerick's wall,
And hurrah ! for bold Sarsfield, the bravest of all.
 But Bradenburgh the ditch has cross'd,
 And gained our flank at little cost—
 The bastion's gone—the town is lost ;
  Oh ! poor city of *Luimneach linn-ghlas.*
 When, sudden, Sarsfield springs the mine—
 Like rockets rise the Germans fine,
 And come down dead, 'mid smoke and shine,
  At the city of *Luimneach linn-ghlas.*

VI.

So, hurrah ! for the men who, when danger is nigh,
Are found in the front, looking death in the eye.
Hurrah ! for the men who kept Limerick's wall,
And hurrah ! for bold Sarsfield, the bravest of all.

Out, with a roar, the Irish sprung,
And back the beaten English flung,
Till William fled, his lords among,
  From the city of *Luimneach linn-ghlas.*
'Twas thus was fought that glorious fight,
By Irishmen, for Ireland's right—
May all such days have such a night
  As the battle of *Luimneach linn-ghlas.*

PART IV.

HISTORICAL BALLADS AND SONGS.

Second Series.

"By a Ballad History we do not mean a metrical chronicle, or any continued work, but a string of ballads chronologically arranged, and illustrating the main events of Irish History, its characters, costumes, scenes, and passions.

"Exact dates, subtle plots, minute connexions and motives, rarely appear in Ballads; and for these ends the worst prose history is superior to the best Ballad series; but these are not the highest ends of history. To hallow or accurse the scenes of glory and honour, or of shame and and sorrow—to give to the imagination the arms, and homes, and senates, and battles of other days—to rouse, and soften, and strengthen, and enlarge us with the passions of great periods—to lead us into love of self-denial, of justice, of beauty, of valour, of generous life, and proud death—and to set up in our souls the memory of great men, who shall then be as models and judges of our actions—these are the highest duties of History, and these are best taught by a Ballad History."— DAVIS'S ESSAYS.

PART IV.

BALLADS AND SONGS ILLUSTRATIVE OF IRISH HISTORY.

THE PENAL DAYS.

AIR.—*The Wheelwright.*

I.

Oh ! weep those days, the penal days,
  When Ireland hopelessly complained.
Oh ! weep those days, the penal days,
  When godless persecution reigned ;
    When year by year,
    For serf, and peer,
  Fresh cruelties were made by law,
    And, filled with hate,
    Our senate sate
  To weld anew each fetter's flaw.
Oh ! weep those days, those penal days—
Their memory still on Ireland weighs.

II.

They bribed the flock, they bribed the son,
  To sell the priest and rob the sire ;
Their dogs were taught alike to run
  Upon the scent of wolf and friar.

K

Among the poor,
Or on the moor,
Were hid the pious and the true—
While traitor knave,
And recreant slave,
Had riches, rank, and retinue ;
And, exiled in those penal days,
Our banners over Europe blaze.

III.

A stranger held the land and tower
Of many a noble fugitive ;
No Popish lord had lordly power,
The peasant scarce had leave to live ;
Above his head
A ruined shed,
No tenure but a tyrant's will—
Forbid to plead,
Forbid to read,
Disarmed, disfranchised, imbecile—
What wonder if our step betrays
The freedman, born in penal days ?

IV.

They're gone, they're gone, those penal days !
All creeds are equal in our isle ;
Then grant, O Lord, thy plenteous grace,
Our ancient feuds to reconcile.
Let all atone
For blood and groan,

For dark revenge and open wrong ;
 Let all unite
 For Ireland's right,
And drown our griefs in freedom's song ;
Till time shall veil in twilight haze,
The memory of those penal days.

THE DEATH OF SARSFIELD.*

A CHANT OF THE BRIGADE.

I.

SARSFIELD has sailed from Limerick Town,
He held it long for country and crown ;
And ere he yielded, the Saxon swore
To spoil our homes and our shrines no more.

II.

Sarsfield and all his chivalry
Are fighting for France in the low countrie—
At his fiery charge the Saxons reel ;
They learned at Limerick to dread the steel.

---

* Sarsfield was slain on the 29th July, 1693, at Landen, heading his countrymen in the van of victory,—King William flying. He could not have died better. His last thoughts were for his country. As he lay on the field unhelmed and dying, he put his hand to his breast. When he took it away, it was full of his best blood. Looking at it sadly with an eye in which victory shone a moment before, he said faintly, " Oh ! that this were for Ireland." He said no more ; and history records no nobler saying, nor any more becoming death.—AUTHOR'S NOTE.—*Vide* Appendix xiv, for a brief sketch of the services of the Irish Brigade, in which most of the allusions in these and several of the following poems are explained.

III.

Sarsfield is dying on Landen's plain !
His corslet had met the ball in vain—
As his life-blood gushes into his hand,
He says, " Oh ! that this was for father-land !"

IV.

Sarsfield is dead, yet no tears shed we—
For he died in the arms of Victory,
And his dying words shall edge the brand,
When we chase the foe from our native land !

THE SURPRISE OF CREMONA.

1702.

I.

FROM Milan to Cremona Duke Villeroy rode,
And soft are the beds in his princely abode ;
In billet and barrack the garrison sleep,
And loose is the watch which the sentinels keep :
'Tis the eve of St. David, and bitter the breeze
Of that mid-winter night on the flat Cremonese ;
A fig for precaution !—Prince Eugene sits down
In winter cantonments round Mantua town !

II.

Yet through Ustiano, and out on the plain,
Horse, foot, and dragoons, are defiling amain.
"That flash !" said Prince Eugene : " Count Merci,
    push on"—
Like a rock from a precipice Merci is gone.

Proud mutters the Prince : " That is Cassioli's sign :
Ere the dawn of the morning Cremona 'll be mine ;
For Merci will open the gate of the Po,
But scant is the mercy Prince Vaudemont will shew !"

III.

Through gate, street, and square, with his keen cava-
    liers—
A flood through a gulley—Count Merci careers—
They ride without getting or giving a blow,
Nor halt till they gaze on the gate of the Po.
" Surrender the gate !"—but a volley replied,
For a handful of Irish are posted inside.
By my faith, Charles Vaudemont will come rather
    late,
If he stay till Count Merci shall open that gate !

IV.

But in through St. Margaret's the Austrians pour,
And billet and barrack are ruddy with gore ;
Unarmed and naked, the soldiers are slain—
There's an enemy's gauntlet on Villeroy's rein—
" A thousand pistoles and a regiment of horse—
Release me, MacDonnell !"—they hold on their course.
Count Merci has seized upon cannon and wall,
Prince Eugene's head-quarters are in the Town-hall !

V.

Here and there, through the city, some readier band,
For honour and safety, undauntedly stand.
At the head of the regiments of Dillon and Burke
Is Major O'Mahony, fierce as a Turk.

His sabre is flashing—the major is dress'd,
But muskets and shirts are the clothes of the rest !
Yet they rush to the ramparts, the clocks have tolled ten
And Count Merci retreats with the half of his men.

VI.

" In on them !" said Friedberg—and Dillon is broke,
Like forest-flowers crushed by the fall of the oak ;
Through the naked battalions the cuirassiers go ;—
But the man, not the dress, makes the soldier, I trow.
Upon them with grapple, with bay'net, and ball,
Like wolves upon gaze-hounds, the Irishmen fall—
Black Friedberg is slain by O'Mahony's steel,
And back from the bullets the cuirassiers reel.

VII.

Oh ! hear you their shout in your quarters, Eugene ?
In vain on Prince Vaudemont for succour you lean !
The bridge has been broken, and, mark ! how, pell-mell,
Come riderless horses, and volley, and yell !—
He's a veteran soldier—he clenches his hands,
He springs on his horse, disengages his bands—
He rallies, he urges, till, hopeless of aid,
He is chased through the gates by the IRISH BRIGADE.

VIII.

News, news, in Vienna !—King Leopold's sad.
News, news, in St. James's !—King William is mad.
News, news, in Versailles !—" Let the Irish Brigade
Be loyally honoured, and royally paid."
News, news, in old Ireland !—high rises her pride,
And high sounds her wail for her children who died,
And deep is her prayer : " God send I may see
MacDonnell and Mahony fighting for me !"

THE FLOWER OF FINAE.

I.

Bright red is the sun on the waves of Lough Sheelin
A cool, gentle breeze from the mountain is stealing,
While fair round its islets the small ripples play,
But fairer than all is the Flower of Finae.

II.

Her hair is like night, and her eyes like grey morning,
She trips on the heather as if its touch scorning,
Yet her heart and her lips are as mild as May day,
Sweet Eily MacMahon, the Flower of Finae.

III.

But who down the hill-side than red deer runs fleeter?
And who on the lake side is hastening to greet her?
Who but Fergus O'Farrell, the fiery and gay,
The darling and pride of the Flower of Finae?

IV.

One kiss and one clasp, and one wild look of gladness;
Ah! why do they change on a sudden to sadness?—
He has told his hard fortune, no more he can stay,
He must leave his poor Eily to pine at Finae.

V.

For Fergus O'Farrell was true to his sire-land,
And the dark hand of tyranny drove him from Ireland;
He joins the Brigade, in the wars far away,
But he vows he'll come back to the Flower of Finae.

VI.

He fought at Cremona—she hears of his story ;
He fought at Cassano—she's proud of his glory ;
Yet sadly she sings *Siúbhail a rúin** all the day,
" Oh ! come, come, my darling, come home to Finae."

VII.

Eight long years have passed, till she's nigh broken-
      hearted,
Her *reel*, and her *rock*, and her *flax* she has parted ;
She sails with the " Wild Geese" to Flanders away,
And leaves her sad parents alone in Finae.

VIII.

Lord Clare on the field of Ramillies is charging—
Before him, the Sacsanach squadrons enlarging—
Behind him the Cravats their sections display—
Beside him rides Fergus and shouts for Finae.

IX.

On the slopes of La Judoigne the Frenchmen are
      flying,
Lord Clare and his squadrons the foe still defying,
Outnumbered, and wounded, retreat in array ;
And bleeding rides Fergus and thinks of Finae.

X.

In the cloisters of Ypres a banner is swaying,
And by it a pale, weeping maiden is praying ;
That flag's the sole trophy of Ramillies' fray ;
This nun is poor Eily, the Flower of Finae.

* Shule aroon.

THE GIRL I LEFT BEHIND ME.

I.

THE dames of France are fond and free,
  And Flemish lips are willing,
And soft the maids of Italy,
  And Spanish eyes are thrilling;
Still, though I bask beneath their smile,
  Their charms fail to bind me,
And my heart flies back to Erin's isle,
  To the girl I left behind me.

II.

For she's as fair as Shannon's side,
  And purer than its water,
But she refused to be my bride,
  Though many a year I sought her;
Yet since to France I sailed away,
  Her letters oft remind me
That I promised never to gainsay
  The girl I left behind me.

III.

She says—"My own dear love, come home,
  My friends are rich and many,
Or else abroad with you I'll roam
  A soldier stout as any;
If you'll not come, nor let me go,
  I'll think you have resigned me."
My heart nigh broke when I answered—No!
  To the girl I left behind me.

IV.

For never shall my true love brave
  A life of war and toiling ;
And never as a skulking slave
  I'll tread my native soil on ;
But, were it free or to be freed,
  The battle's close would find me
To Ireland bound—nor message need
  From the girl I left behind me.

CLARE'S DRAGOONS.*

AIR.—*Viva la*

I.

WHEN, on Ramillies' bloody field,
The baffled French were forced to yield,
The victor Saxon backward reeled
  Before the charge of Clare's Dragoons.
The Flags, we conquered in that fray,
Look lone in Ypres' choir, they say,
We'll win them company to-day,
  Or bravely die like Clare's Dragoons.

CHORUS.

Viva la, for Ireland's wrong !
  Viva la, for Ireland's right !
Viva la, in battle throng,
  For a Spanish steed, and sabre bright !

* *Vide* Appendix xlv.

II.

The brave old lord died near the fight,
But, for each drop he lost that night,
A Saxon cavalier shall bite
    The dust before Lord Clare's Dragoons.
For, never, when our spurs were set,
And never, when our sabres met,
Could we the Saxon soldiers get
    To stand the shock of Clare's Dragoons.

CHORUS.

Viva la, the New Brigade !
    Viva la, the Old One, too !
Viva la, the rose shall fade,
    And the shamrock shine for ever new !

III.

Another Clare is here to lead,
The worthy son of such a breed ;
The French expect some famous deed,
    When Clare leads on his bold Dragoons.
Our colonel comes from Brian's race,
His wounds are in his breast and face,
The *bearna baoghail** is still his place,
    The foremost of his bold Dragoons.

CHORUS.

Viva la, the New Brigade !
    Viva la, the Old One, too !
Viva la, the rose shall fade,
    And the Shamrock shine for ever new !

* Gap of danger.

IV.

There's not a man in squadron here
Was ever known to flinch or fear ;
Though first in charge and last in rere,
  Have ever been Lord Clare's Dragoons ;
But, see ! we'll soon have work to do,
To shame our boasts, or prove them true,
For hither comes the English crew,
  To sweep away Lord Clare's Dragoons.

CHORUS.

Viva la, for Ireland's wrong !
  Viva la, for Ireland's right !
Viva la, in battle throng,
  For a Spanish steed and sabre bright !

V.

Oh ! comrades ! think how Ireland pines,
Her exiled lords, her rifled shrines,
Her dearest hope, the ordered lines,
  And bursting charge of Clare's Dragoons.
Then fling your Green Flag to the sky,
Be Limerick your battle-cry,
And charge, till blood floats fetlock-high,
  Around the track of Clare's Dragoons !

CHORUS.

Viva la, the New Brigade !
  Viva la, the Old One, too !
Viva la, the rose shall fade,
  And the Shamrock shine for ever new !

WHEN SOUTH WINDS BLOW.

Air.—*The gentle Maiden.*

I.

WHY sits the gentle maiden there,
  While surfing billows splash around ?
Why doth she southwards wildly stare,
  And sing, with such a fearful sound—
"The Wild Geese fly where others walk ;
The Wild Geese do what others talk—
The way is long from France, you know—
He'll come at last when south winds blow."

II.

Oh ! softly was the maiden nurst
  In Castle Connell's lordly towers,
Where Skellig's billows boil and burst,
  And, far above, Dunkerron towers ;
And she was noble as the hill—
Yet battle-flags are nobler still :
And she was graceful as the wave—
Yet who would live a tranquil slave ?

III.

And, so, her lover went to France,
  To serve the foe of Ireland's foe ;
Yet deep he swore—"Whatever chance,
  "I'll come some day when south winds blow."

And prouder hopes he told beside,
How she should be a prince's bride,
How Louis would the Wild Geese* send,
And Ireland's weary woes should end.

IV.

But tyrants quenched her father's hearth,
    And wrong and absence warped her mind ;
The gentle maid, of gentle birth,
    Is moaning madly to the wind—·
" He said he'd come, whate'er betide ;
He said I'd be a happy bride ;
Oh ! long the way and hard the foe—
He'll come when south—when south winds blow !"

THE BATTLE EVE OF THE BRIGADE.

Air—*Contented I am.*

I.

The mess-tent is full, and the glasses are set,
And the gallant Count Thomond is president yet ;
The vet'ran arose, like an uplifted lance,
Crying—" Comrades, a health to the monarch of
      France !"
With bumpers and cheers they have done as he bade,
For King Louis is loved by The Irish Brigade.

* The recruiting for the Brigade was carried on in the French ships
which smuggled brandies, wines, silks, &c., to the western and south-
western coasts. Their return cargoes were recruits for the Brigade, and
were entered in their books as Wild Geese. Hence this became the
common name in Ireland for the Irish serving in the Brigade. The
recruiting was chiefly from Clare, Limerick, Cork, Kerry, and Galway.

II.

"A health to King James," and they bent as they
    quaffed,
"Here's to George the *Elector*," and fiercely they
    laughed,
"Good luck to the girls we wooed long ago,
Where Shannon, and Barrow, and Blackwater flow;"
"God prosper Old Ireland,"—you'd think them afraid,
So pale grew the chiefs of The Irish Brigade.

III.

"But, surely, that light cannot come from our lamp?
And that noise—are they *all* getting drunk in the
    camp?"
"Hurrah! boys, the morning of battle is come,
And the *generale's* beating on many a drum."
So they rush from the revel to join the parade:
For the van is the right of The Irish Brigade.

IV.

They fought as they revelled, fast, fiery, and true,
And, though victors, they left on the field not a few;
And they, who survived, fought and drank as of
    yore,
But the land of their heart's hope they never saw
    more;
For in far foreign fields, from Dunkirk to Belgrade,
Lie the soldiers and chiefs of The Irish Brigade.

FONTENOY.*

1745.

I.

THRICE, at the huts of Fontenoy, the English column
    failed,
And, twice, the lines of Saint Antoine, the Dutch in
    vain assailed ;
For town and slope were filled with fort and flanking
    battery,
And well they swept the English ranks, and Dutch
    auxiliary.
As vainly, through De Barri's wood, the British
    soldiers burst,
The French artillery drove them back, diminished,
    and dispersed.
The bloody Duke of Cumberland beheld with anxious
    eye,
And ordered up his last reserve, his latest chance to
    try,
On Fontenoy, on Fontenoy, how fast his generals
    ride !
And mustering come his chosen troops, like clouds at
    eventide.

II.

Six thousand English veterans in stately column
    tread,
Their cannon blaze in front and flank, Lord Hay is at
    their head ;

* *Vide* Appendix xiv.

Steady they step a-down the slope—steady they climb
   the hill ;
Steady they load—steady they fire, moving right on-
   ward still,
Betwixt the wood and Fontenoy, as through a furnace
   blast,
Through rampart, trench, and palisade, and bullets
   showering fast ;
And on the open plain above they rose, and kept
   their course,
With ready fire and grim resolve, that mocked at
   hostile force :
Past Fontenoy, past Fontenoy, while thinner grow
   their ranks—
They break, as broke the Zuyder Zee through Holland's ocean banks.

III.

More idly than the summer flies, French tirailleurs
   rush round ;
As stubble to the lava tide, French squadrons strew
   the ground ;
Bomb-shell, and grape, and round-short tore, still on
   they marched and fired—
Fast, from each volley, grenadier and voltigeur retired.
"Push on, my household cavalry !" King Louis madly
   cried :
To death they rush, but rude their shock—not unavenged they died.
On through the camp the column trod—King Louis
   turns his rein :
"Not yet, my liege," Saxe interposed, "the Irish
   troops remain ;"

And Fontenoy, famed Fontenoy, had been a Waterloo,
Were not these exiles ready then, fresh, vehement,
and true.

IV.

"Lord Clare," he says, "you have your wish; there
are your Saxon foes!"
The Marshal almost smiles to see, so furiously he
goes!
How fierce the look these exiles wear, who're wont to
be so gay,
The treasured wrongs of fifty years are in their hearts
to-day—
The treaty broken, ere the ink wherewith 'twas writ
could dry,
Their plundered homes, their ruined shrines, their
women's parting cry,
Their priesthood hunted down like wolves, their country overthrown—
Each looks as if revenge for all were staked on him
alone.
On Fontenoy, on Fontenoy, nor ever yet elsewhere,
Rushed on to fight a nobler band than these proud
exiles were.

V.

O'Brien's voice is hoarse with joy, as, halting, he
commands,
"Fix bay'nets!—charge!" Like mountain storm,
rush on these fiery bands!
Thin is the English column now, and faint their
volleys grow,
Yet, must'ring all the strength they have, they make
a gallant show.

They dress their ranks upon the hill to face that
battle-wind—
Their bayonets the breakers' foam ; like rocks, the
men behind !
One volley crashes from their line, when, through
the surging smoke,
With empty guns clutched in their hands, the head-
long Irish broke.
On Fontenoy, on Fontenoy, hark to that fierce huzza !
" Revenge ! remember Limerick ! dash down the
Sacsanach !"

VI.

Like lions leaping at a fold, when mad with hunger's
pang,
Right up against the English line the Irish exiles
sprang :
Bright was their steel, 'tis bloody now, their guns are
filled with gore ;
Through shattered ranks, and severed files, the
trampled flags they tore ;
The English strove with desperate strength, paused,
rallied, staggered, fled—
The green hill-side is matted close with dying and
with dead.
Across the plain, and far away passed on that hideous
wrack,
While cavalier and fantassin dash in upon their track.
On Fontenoy, on Fontenoy, like eagles in the sun,
With bloody plumes, the Irish stand—the field is
fought and won !

THE DUNGANNON CONVENTION

1782.

I.

THE church of Dungannon is full to the door,
And sabre and spur clash at times on the floor,
While helmet and shako are ranged all along,
Yet no book of devotion is seen in the throng.
In the front of the altar no minister stands,
But the crimson-clad chief of these warrior bands;
And, though solemn the looks and the voices around,
You'd listen in vain for a litany's sound.
Say! what do they hear in the temple of prayer?
Oh! why in the fold has the lion his lair?

II.

Sad, wounded, and wan was the face of our isle,
By English oppression, and falsehood, and guile;
Yet when to invade it a foreign fleet steered,
To guard it for England the North volunteered.
From the citizen-soldiers the foe fled aghast—
Still they stood to their guns when the danger had past,
For the voice of America came o'er the wave,
Crying: Woe to the tyrant, and hope to the slave!
Indignation and shame through their regiments speed:
They have arms in their hands, and what more do
      they need?

III.

O'er the green hills of Ulster their banners are spread,
The cities of Leinster resound to their tread,

The valleys of Munster with ardour are stirred,
And the plains of wild Connaught their bugles have
    heard ;
A Protestant front-rank and Catholic rere—
For—forbidden the arms of freemen to bear—
Yet foeman and friend are full sure, if need be,
The slave for his country will stand by the free.
By green flags supported, the Orange flags wave,
And the soldier half turns to unfetter the slave !

IV.

More honoured that church of Dungannon is now,
Than when at its altar communicants bow ;
More welcome to heaven than anthem or prayer,
Are the rites and the thoughts of the warriors there ;
In the name of all Ireland the Delegates swore :
" We've suffered too long, and we'll suffer no more—
Unconquered by Force, we were vanquished by Fraud ;
And now, in God's temple, we vow unto God,
That never again shall the Englishman bind
His chains on our limbs, or his laws on our mind."

V.

The church of Dungannon is empty once more—
No plumes on the altar, no clash on the floor,
But the councils of England are fluttered to see,
In the cause of their country, the Irish agree ;
So they give as a boon what they dare not withhold,
And Ireland, a nation, leaps up as of old,
With a name, and a trade, and a flag of her own,
And an army to fight for the people and throne.
But woe worth the day if to falsehood or fears
She surrenders the guns of her brave Volunteers !

SONG OF THE VOLUNTEERS OF 1782.

Air—The Boyne Water.

I.

HURRAH ! 'tis done —our freedom's won—
    Hurrah ! for the Volunteers !
No laws we own, but those alone
    Of our Commons, King, and Peers.
The chain is broke—the Saxon yoke
    From off our neck is taken ;
Ireland awoke—Dungannon spoke—
    With fear was England shaken.

II.

When Grattan rose, none dared oppose
    The claim he made for freedom :
They knew our swords, to back his words,
    Were ready, did he need them.
Then let us raise, to Grattan's praise,
    A proud and joyous anthem ;
And wealth, and grace, and length of days,
    May God, in mercy, grant him !

III.

Bless Harry Flood, who nobly stood
    By us, through gloomy years !
Bless Charlemont, the brave and good,
    The Chief of the Volunteers !
The North began ; the North held on
    The strife for native land ;
Till Ireland rose, and cowed her foes—
    God bless the Northern land !

IV.

And bless the men of patriot pen—
 Swift, Molyneux, and Lucas ;
Bless sword and gun, which " Free Trade " won,
 Bless God ! who ne'er forsook us !
And long may last, the friendship fast,
 Which binds us all together ;
While we agree, our foes shall flee
 Like clouds in stormy weather.

V

Remember still, through good and ill,
 How vain were prayers and tears—
How vain were words, till flashed the swords
 Of the Irish Volunteers.
By arms we've got the rights we sought
 Through long and wretched years—
Hurrah ! 'tis done, our Freedom's won—
 Hurrah ! for the Volunteers !

THE MEN OF 'EIGHTY-TWO.

AIR—*An Cruisgin Lan.*

I.

To rend a cruel chain,
To end a foreign reign,
The swords of the Volunteers were drawn,
 And instant from their sway,
 Oppression fled away ;
So we'll drink them in a *cruisgin lán, lán, lán,*
We'll drink them in a *cruisgin lán !*

II.

Within that host were seen
The Orange, Blue, and Green—
The Bishop for its coat left his lawn—
The peasant and the lord
Ranked in with one accord,
Like brothers at a *cruisgin lán, lán, lán,*
Like brothers at a *cruisgin lán !.*

III.

With liberty there came
Wit, eloquence, and fame ;
Our feuds went like mists from the dawn ;
Old bigotry disdained—
Old privilege retained—
Oh ! sages, fill a *cruisgin lán, lán, lán,*
And, boys ! fill up a *cruisgin lán !*

IV.

The trader's coffers filled,
The barren lands were tilled,
Our ships on the waters thick as spawn—
Prosperity broke forth,
Like summer in the north—
Ye merchants ! fill a *cruisgin lán, lán, lán,*
Ye farmers ! fill a *cruisgin lán !*

V.

The memory of that day
Shall never pass away,
Tho' its fame shall be yet outshone ;

We'll grave it on our shrines,
We'll shout it in our lines—
Old Ireland! fill a *crúisgín lán, lán, lán,*
Young Ireland! fill a *crúisgín lán !*

VI.

And drink—The Volunteers,
Their generals, and seers,
Their gallantry, their genius, and their brawn,
With water, or with wine—
The draught is but a sign—
The purpose fills the *crúisgín lán, lán, lán,*
This purpose fills the *crúisgín lán !*

VII.

That, ere Old Ireland goes,
And while Young Ireland glows,
The swords of our sires be girt on,
And loyally renew
The work of 'EIGHTY-Two—
Oh! gentlemen—a *crúisgín lán, lán, lán,*
Our freedom! in a *crúisgín lán !*

NATIVE SWORDS.

A VOLUNTEER SONG.—1ST JULY, 1792.

Air—*Boyne Water.*

I.

We've bent too long to braggart wrong,
  While force our prayers derided :
We've fought too long, ourselves among,
  By knaves and priests divided.
United now, no more we'll bow,
  Foul faction we discard it ;
And now, thank God ! our native sod
  Has Native Swords to guard it.

II.

Like rivers, which, o'er valleys rich,
  Bring ruin in their water,
On native land, a native hand
  Flung foreign fraud and slaughter.
From Dermod's crime to Tudor's time
  Our clans were our perdition ;
Religion's name, since then, became
  Our pretext for division.

III.

But, worse than all, with Lim'rick's fall
  Our valour seem'd to perish ;
Or, o'er the main, in France and Spain,
  For bootless vengeance flourish.
The peasant here grew pale, for fear
  He'd suffer for our glory,
While France sang joy for Fontenoy,
  And Europe hymned our story.

IV.

But, now, no clan, nor factious plan,
    The East and West can sunder—
Why Ulster e'er should Munster fear,
    Can only wake our wonder.
Religion's crost, when union's lost,
    And " royal gifts " retard it ;
But now, thank God ! our native sod
    Has Native Swords to guard it.

TONE'S GRAVE.

I.

In Bodenstown Churchyard there is a green grave,
And wildly along it the winter winds rave ;
Small shelter, I ween, are the ruined walls there,
When the storm sweeps down on the plains of Kildare.

II.

Once I lay on that sod—it lies over Wolfe Tone—
And thought how he perished in prison alone,
His friends unavenged, and his country unfreed—
" Oh, bitter," I said, " is the patriot's meed ;

III.

For in him the heart of a woman combined
With a heroic life, and a governing mind—
A martyr for Ireland—his grave has no stone—
His name seldom named, and his virtues unknown."

IV.

I was woke from my dream by the voices and tread
Of a band, who came into the home of the dead ;
They carried no corpse, and they carried no stone,
And they stopped when they came to the grave of
    Wolf Tone.

V.

There were students and peasants, the wise and the
    brave,
And an old man who knew him from cradle to grave,
And children who thought me hard-hearted ; for they,
On that sanctified sod, were forbidden to play.

VI.

But the old man, who saw I was mourning there, said :
" We come, sir, to weep where young Wolfe Tone is
    laid,
And we're going to raise him a monument, too--
A plain one, yet fit for the simple and true."

VII.

My heart overflowed, and I clasped his old hand,
And I blessed him, and blessed every one of his band :
" Sweet ! sweet ! 'tis to find that such faith can remain
To the cause, and the man so long vanquished and
    slain."

VIII.

In Bodenstown Churchyard there is a green grave,
And freely around it let winter winds rave—
Far better they suit him—the ruin and gloom,—
TILL IRELAND, A NATION, CAN BUILD HIM A TOMB.

PART V.

MISCELLANEOUS POEMS.

"NATIONALITY is no longer an unmeaning or despised name among us. It is welcomed by the higher ranks, it is the inspiration of the bold, and the hope of the people. It is the summary name for many things. It seeks a Literature made by Irishmen, and coloured by our scenery, manners, and character. It desires to see Art applied to express Irish thoughts and belief. It would make our Music sound in every parish at twilight, our Pictures sprinkle the walls of every house, and our Poetry and History sit at every hearth.

"It would thus create a race of men full of a more intensely Irish character and knowledge, and to that race it would give Ireland. It would give them the seas of Ireland to sweep with their nets and launch on with their navy; the harbours of Ireland, to receive a greater commerce than any island in the world; the soil of Ireland to live on, by more millions than starve here now; the fame of Ireland to enhance by their genius and valour; the Independence of Ireland to guard by laws and arms."—DAVIS'S ESSAYS.

PART V.

MISCELLANEOUS POEMS.

——•——

NATIONALITY.

I.

A NATION'S voice, a nation's voice--
   It is a solemn thing !
It bids the bondage-sick rejoice—
   'Tis stronger than a king.
'Tis like the light of many stars,
   The sound of many waves ;
Which brightly look through prison-bars ;
   And sweetly sound in caves.
Yet is it noblest, godliest known,
When righteous triumph swells its tone.

II.

A nation's flag, a nation's flag—
   If wickedly unrolled,
May foes in adverse battle drag
   Its every fold from fold.
But in the cause of Liberty,
   Guard it 'gainst Earth and Hell ;

Guard it till Death or Victory—
 Look you, you guard it well !
No saint or king has tomb so proud,
As he whose flag becomes his shroud.

III.

A nation's right, a nation's right—
 God gave it, and gave, too.
A nation's sword, a nation's might,
 Danger to guard it through.
'Tis freedom from a foreign yoke,
 'Tis just and equal laws,
Which deal unto the humblest folk,
 As in a noble's cause.
On nation's fixed in right and truth,
God would bestow eternal youth.

IV

May Ireland's voice be ever heard
 Amid the world's applause !
And never be her flag-staff stirred,
 But in an honest cause !
May freedom be her very breath,
 Be Justice ever dear ;
And never an ennobled death
 May son of Ireland fear !
So the Lord God will ever smile,
With guardian grace, upon our isle.

SELF-RELIANCE.

I.

THOUGH savage force and subtle schemes,
　And alien rule, through ages lasting,
Have swept your land like lava streams,
　Its wealth, and name, and nature blasting ;
Rot not, therefore, in dull despair,
　Nor moan at destiny in far lands !
Face not your foe with bosom bare,
　Nor hide your chains in pleasure's garlands.
The wise man arms to combat wrong,
　The brave man clears a den of lions,
The true man spurns the Helot's song ;
　The freeman's friend is Self-Reliance !

II.

Though France, that gave your exiles bread,
　Your priests a home, your hopes a station,
Or that young land where first was spread
　The starry flag of Liberation,—
Should heed your wrongs some future day,
　And send you voice or sword to plead 'em,
With helpful love their help repay,
　But trust not even to them for Freedom.
A Nation freed by foreign aid
　Is but a corpse by wanton science
Convulsed like life, then flung to fade—
　The life itself is Self-Reliance !

M

III.

Oh ! see your quailing tyrant run
    To courteous lies, and Roman agents ;
His terror, lest Dungannon's sun
    Should rise again with riper radiance.
Oh ! hark the Freeman's welcome cheer,
    And hark your brother sufferers sobbing ;
Oh ! mark the universe grow clear,
    And mark your spirit's royal throbbing—
'Tis Freedom's God that sends such signs,
    As pledges of his blest alliance ;
He gives bright hopes to brave designs,
    And lends his bolts to Self-Reliance !

IV.

Then, flung alone, or hand in hand,
    In mirthful hour, or spirit solemn ;
In lowly toil, or high command,
    In social hall, or charging column :
In tempting wealth, and trying woe,
    In struggling with a mob's dictation ;
In bearing back a foreign foe,
    In training up a troubled nation :
Still hold to Truth, abound in Love,
    Refusing every base compliance—
Your Praise within, your Prize above,
    And live and die in SELF-RELIANCE !

SWEET AND SAD.

A PRISON SERMON.

I.

'Tis sweet to climb the mountain's crest,
And run, like deer-hound, down its breast ;
'Tis sweet to snuff the taintless air,
And sweep the sea with haughty stare :
And, sad it is, when iron bars
Keep watch between you and the stars ;
And sad to find your footstep stayed
By prison-wall and palisade ;
    But 'twere better be
      A prisoner for ever,
    With no destiny
      To do, or to endeavour ;
    Better life to spend
      A martyr or confessor,
    Than in silence bend
      To alien and oppressor.

II.

'Tis sweet to rule an ample realm,
Through weal and woe to hold the helm ;
And sweet to strew, with plenteous hand,
Strength, health, and beauty, round your land :
And sad it is to be unprized,
While dotards rule, unrecognized ;
And sad your little ones to see
Writhe in the gripe of poverty :

But 'twere better pine
  In rags and gnawing hunger,
While around you whine
  Your elder and your younger ;
Better lie in pain,
  And rise in pain to-morrow,
Than o'er millions reign,
  While those millions sorrow.

III.

'Tis sweet to own a quiet hearth,
Begirt by constancy and mirth ;
'Twere sweet to feel your dying clasp
Returned by friendship's steady grasp :
And sad it is to spend your life,
Like sea-lird in the ceaseless strife—
Your lullaby the ocean's roar,
Your resting-place a foreign shore :
    But 'twere better live,
      Like ship caught by Lofoden,
    Than your spirit give
      To be by chains corroden ;
    Best of all to yield
      Your latest breath, when lying
    On a victor field,
      With the green flag flying !

IV.

Human joy and human sorrow,
Light or shade from conscience borrow ;
The tyrant's crown is lined with flame,
Life never paid the coward's shame :

The miser's lock is never sure,
The traitor's home is never pure ;
While seraphs guard, and cherubs tend
The good man's life and brave man's end :
But their fondest care
Is the patriot's prison,
Hymning through its air—
" Freedom hath arisen,
Oft from statesmen's strife,
Oft from battle's flashes,
Oft from hero's life,
Oftenest from his ashes !"

THE BURIAL.*

WHY rings the knell of the funeral bell from a hundred village shrines ?
Through broad Fingall, where hasten all those long and ordered lines ?
With tear and sigh they're passing by—the matron and the maid—
Has a hero died—is a nation's pride in that cold coffin laid ?
With frown and curse, behind the hearse, dark men go tramping on—
Has a tyrant died, that they cannot hide their wrath till the rites are done ?

---

* Written on the funeral of the Rev. P. J. Tyrrell, P.P., of Lusk ; one of those indicted with O'Connell in the government prosecution of 1843.

THE CHANT.

" *Ululu ! ululu !* high on the wind,
" There's a home for the slave where no fetters can
     bind.
" Woe, woe to his slayers !"—comes wildly along,
With the trampling of feet and the funeral song.

    And now more clear
    It swells on the ear ;
    Breathe low, and listen, 'tis solemn to hear.

" *Ululu ! ululu !* wail for the dead.
" Green grow the grass of Fingall on his head ;
" And spring-flowers blossom, ere elsewhere appear-
    ing,
" And shamrocks grow thick on the Martyr for Erin.
" *Ululu ! ululu !* soft fall the dew
" On the feet and the head of the martyred and true."

    For awhile they tread
    In silence dread—
    Then muttering and moaning go the crowd,
    Surging and swaying like mountain cloud,
    And again the wail comes fearfully loud.

THE CHANT.

" *Ululu ! ululu !* kind was his heart !
" Walk slower, walk slower, too soon we shall part.
" The faithful and pious, the Priest of the Lord,
" His pilgrimage over, he has his reward.
" By the bed of the sick, lowly kneeling,
" To God with the raised cross appealing—

" He seems still to kneel, and he seems still to pray,
" And the sins of the dying seem passing away.

" In the prisoner's cell, and the cabin so dreary,
" Our constant consoler, he never grew weary ;
" But he's gone to his rest,
" And he's now with the bless'd,
" Where tyrant and traitor no longer molest—
" *Ululu ! ululu !* wail for the dead !
" *Ululu ! ululu !* here is his bed !"

Short was the ritual, simple the prayer,
Deep was the silence and every head bare :
The Priest alone standing, they knelt all around,
Myriads on myriads, like rocks on the ground.
Kneeling and motionless—" Dust unto dust."
" He died as becometh the faithful and just—
" Placing in God his reliance and trust ;"

Kneeling and motionless—" ashes to ashes "—
Hollow the clay on the coffin-lid dashes ;
Kneeling and motionless, wildly they pray,
But they pray in their souls, for no gesture have they :
Stern and standing—oh ! look on them now,
Like trees to one tempest the multitude bow ;
Like the swell of the ocean is rising their vow :

THE VOW.

" We have bent and borne, though we saw him torn
    from his home by the tyrant's crew—
" And we bent and bore, when he came once more,
    though suffering had pierced him through :

" And now he is laid beyond our aid, because to Ire
    land true—
" A martyred man—the tyrant's ban, the pious patriot
    slew.

    " And shall we bear and bend for ever,
    " And shall no time our bondage sever,
    " And shall we kneel, but battle never,
               " For our own soil ?
    " And shall our tyrants safely reign
    " On thrones built up of slaves and slain,
    " And nought to us and ours remain
               " But chains and toil ?
    " No ! round this grave our oath we plight,
    " To watch, and labour, and unite,
    " Till banded be the nation's might—
               " Its spirit steeled,
    " And then, collecting all our force,
    " We'll cross oppression in its course,
    " And die—or all our rights enforce,
               " On battle field."

Like an ebbing sea that will come again,
Slowly retired that host of men ;
Methinks they'll keep some other day
The oath they swore on the martyr's clay.

WE MUST NOT FAIL.

I.

We must not fail, we must not fail,
However fraud or force assail ;
By honour, pride, and policy,
By Heaven itself !—we must be free.

II.

Time had already thinned our chain,
Time would have dulled our sense of pain ;
By service long, and suppliance vile,
We might have won our owner's smile.

III.

We spurned the thought, our prison burst,
And dared the despot to the worst ;
Renewed the strife of centuries,
And flung our banner to the breeze.

IV.

We called the ends of earth to view
The gallant deeds we swore to do ;
They knew us wronged, they knew us brave,
And, all we asked, they freely gave.

V.

We took the starving peasant's mite
To aid in winning back his right,
We took the priceless trust of youth ;
Their freedom must redeem our truth.

VI.

We promised loud, and boasted high,
"To break our country's chains, or die ;"
And, should we quail, that country's name
Will be the synonyme of shame.

VII.

Earth is not deep enough to hide
The coward slave who shrinks aside ;
Hell is not hot enough to scathe
The ruffian wretch who breaks his faith.

VIII.

But—calm, my soul !—we promised true
Her destined work our land shall do ;
Thought, courage, patience will prevail !
We shall not fail—we shall not fail !

O'CONNELL'S STATUE.

LINES TO HOGAN.

Chisel the likeness of The Chief,
Not in gaiety, nor grief ;
Change not by your art to stone,
Ireland's laugh, or Ireland's moan.
Dark her tale, and none can tell
Its fearful chronicle so well.
Her frame is bent—her wounds are deep·—
Who, like him, her woes can weep ?

He can be gentle as a bride,
While none can rule with kinglier pride ;
Calm to hear, and wise to prove,
Yet gay as lark in soaring love.
Well it were, posterity
Should have some image of his glee ;
That easy humour, blossoming
Like the thousand flowers of spring !
Glorious the marble which could show
His bursting sympathy for woe :
Could catch the pathos, flowing wild,
Like mother's milk to craving child.

And oh ! how princely were the art
Could mould his mien, or tell his heart.
When sitting sole on Tara's hill,
While hung a million on his will !
Yet, not in gaiety, nor grief,
Chisel the image of our Chief ;
Nor even in that haughty hour
When a nation owned his power.

But would you by your art unroll
His own, and Ireland's secret soul,
And give to other times to scan
The greatest greatness of the man ?
Fierce defiance let him be
Hurling at our enemy.—
From a base as fair and sure,
As our love is true and pure,
Let his statue rise as tall
And firm as a castle wall ;

On his broad brow let there be
A type of Ireland's history ;
Pious, generous, deep, and warm,
Strong and changeful as a storm ;
Let whole centuries of wrong
Upon his recollection throng—
Strongbow's force, and Henry's wile,
Tudor's wrath, and Stuart's guile,
And iron Strafford's tiger jaws,
And brutal Brunswick's penal laws ;
Not forgetting Saxon faith,
Not forgetting Norman scath,
Not forgetting William's word,
Not forgetting Cromwell's sword.
Let the Union's fetter vile—
The shame and ruin of our isle—
Let the blood of 'Ninety-Eight
And our present blighting fate—
Let the poor mechanic's lot,
And the peasant's ruined cot,
Plundered wealth and glory flown,
Ancient honours overthrown—
Let trampled altar, rifled urn,
Knit his look to purpose stern.
Mould all this into one thought,
Like wizard cloud with thunder fraught ;
Still let our glories through it gleam,
Like fair flowers through a flooded stream,
Or like a flashing wave at night,
Bright,—'mid the solemn darkness, bright.
Let the memory of old days
Shine through the statesman's anxious face—
Dathi's power, and Brian's fame,
And headlong Sarsfield's sword of flame ;

And the spirit of Red Hugh,
And the pride of 'Eighty-Two,
And the victories he won,
And the hope that leads him on !

Let whole armies seem to fly
From his threatening hand and eye ;
Be the strength of all the land
Like a falchion in his hand,
And be his gesture sternly grand.
A braggart tyrant swore to smite
A people struggling for their right—
O'Connell dared him to the field,
Content to die, but never yield.
Fancy such a soul as his,
In a moment such as this,
Like cataract, or foaming tide,
Or army charging in its pride.
Thus he spoke, and thus he stood,
Proffering in our cause his blood.
Thus his country loves him best—
To image this is your behest.
Chisel thus, and thus alone,
If to man you'd change the stone.

THE GREEN ABOVE THE RED.*

AIR.--*Irish Molly O!*

I.

FULL often when our fathers saw the Red above the
    Green,
They rose in rude but fierce array, with sabre, pike
    and *scian*,
And over many a noble town, and many a field of
    dead,
They proudly set the Irish Green above the English
    Red.

II.

But in the end throughout the land, the shameful
    sight was seen—
The English Red in triumph high above the Irish
    Green ;
But well they died in breach and field, who, as their
    spirits fled,
Still saw the Green maintain its place above the
    English Red.

III.

And they who saw, in after times, the Red above the
    Green,
Were withered as the grass that dies beneath a forest
    screen ;

---

* This, and the three following pieces are properly street ballads.
The reader must not expect depth or finish in verses of this description,
written for a temporary purpose.- ED.

Yet often by this healthy hope their sinking hearts
    were fed,
That, in some day to come, the Green should flutter
    o'er the Red.

IV.

Sure 'twas for this Lord Edward died, and Wolf Tone
    sunk serene—
Because they could not bear to leave the Red above
    the Green ;
And 'twas for this that Owen fought, and Sarsfield
    nobly bled—
Because their eyes were hot to see the Green above
    the Red.

V.

So when the strife began again, our darling Irish
    Green,
Was down upon the earth, while high the English
    Red was seen ;
Yet still we held our fearless course, for something in
    us said,
" Before the strife is o'er you'll see the Green above
    the Red."

VI.

And 'tis for this we think and toil, and knowledge
    strive to glean,
That we may pull the English Red below the Irish
    Green,
And leave our sons sweet Liberty, and smiling plenty
    spread
Above the land once dark with blood—*the Green
    above the Red !*

VII.

The jealous English tyrant now has banned the Irish
    Green,
And forced us to conceal it like a something foul and
    mean ;
But yet, by Heavens ! he'll sooner raise his victims
    from the dead
Than force our hearts to leave the Green, and cotton
    to the Red !

VIII.

We'll trust ourselves, for God is good, and blesses
    those who lean
On their brave hearts, and not upon an earthly king
    or queen ;
And, freely as we lift our hands, we vow our blood to
    shed
Once and for evermore to raise the Green above the
    Red.

THE VOW OF TIPPERARY.

I.

From Carrick streets to Shannon shore,
    From Slievenamon to Ballindeary,
From Longford Pass to Gaillte Mór,
    Come hear The Vow of Tipperary.

II.

Too long we fought for Britain's cause,
    And of our blood were never chary ;
She paid us back with tyrant laws,
    And thinned The Homes of Tipperary.

III.

Too long, with rash and single arm,
  The peasant strove to guard his eyrie,
Till Irish blood bedewed each farm,
  And Ireland wept for Tipperary.

IV.

But never more we'll lift a hand—
  We swear by God and Virgin Mary !
Except in war for Native Land,
  And *that's* The Vow of Tipperary !

A PLEA FOR THE BOG-TROTTERS.

I.

" Base Bog-trotters," says the *Times,*
" Brown with mud, and black with crimes,
Turf and lumpers dig betimes
    (We grant you need 'em),
But never lift your heads sublime,
    Nor talk of Freedom."

II.

Yet, Bog-trotters, sirs, be sure,
Are strong to do, and to endure,
Men whose blows are hard to cure—
    Brigands ! what's in ye,
That the fierce man of the moor
    Can't stand again ye ?

N

III.

The common drains in Mushra moss
Are wider than a castle fosse,
Connaught swamps are hard to cross,
        And histories boast
That Allen's Bog has caused the loss
        Of many a host.

IV.

Oh ! were you in an Irish bog,
Full of pikes, and scarce of prog,
You'd wish your *Times*-ship was incog.
        Or far away,
Though Saxons, thick as London fog,
        Around you lay.

A SECOND PLEA FOR THE BOG-TROTTERS.

I.

THE *Mail* says, that Hanover's King
Twenty Thousand men will bring,
And make the " base bog-trotters sing
        A *pillieu ;*
And that O'Connell high shall swing,
        And others too.

II.

There is a tale of Athens told,
Worth at least its weight in gold
To fellows of King Ernest's mould,
        (The royal rover),
Who think men may be bought and sold,
        Or ridden over.

III.

Darius (an Imperial wretch
A Persian Ernest, or Jack Ketch,)
Bid his knaves from Athens fetch
    " Earth and water,"
Or else the herald's neck he'd stretch,
    And Athens slaughter.

IV.

The Athenians threw them in a well,
And left them there to help themsel',
And when his armies came, pell-mell,
    They tore his banners,
And sent his slaves in shoals to hell,
    To mend their manners.

V.

Let those who bring and those who send
Hanoverians, comprehend
Persian-like may be their end,
    And the " bog-trotter "
May drown their knaves, their banners rend,
    Their armies slaughter.

A SCENE IN THE SOUTH.

I.

I was walking along in a pleasant place,
    In the county Tipperary ;
The scene smiled as happy as the holy face
    Of the Blessed Virgin Mary ;
And the trees were proud, and the sward was green,
And the birds sang loud in the leafy scene.

II.

Yet somehow I felt strange, and soon I felt sad,
    And then I felt very lonely ;
I pondered in vain why I was not glad,
    In a place meant for pleasure only :
For I thought that grief had never been there,
And that sin would as lief to heaven repair.

III.

And a train of spirits seemed passing me by,
    The air grew as heavy as lead ;
I looked for a cabin, yet none could I spy
    In the pastures about me spread ;
Yet each field seemed made for a peasant's cot,
And I felt dismayed whan I saw them not.

IV.

As I stayed on the field, I saw—Oh, my God !
    The marks where a cabin had been :
Through the midst of the fields, some feet of the
        sod
    Were coarser and far less green,

And three or four trees in the centre stood,
But they seemed to freeze in their solitude.

V.

Surely here was the road that led to the cot,
   For it ends just beneath the trees,
And the trees like mourners are watching the spot,
   And *cronauning* with the breeze;
And their stems are bare with children's play,
But the children—where, oh! where are they?

VI.

An old man unnoticed had come to my side,
   His hand in my arm linking—
A reverend man, without haste or pride—
   And he said:—" I know what you're thinking;
" A cabin stood once underneath the trees,
" Full of kindly ones—but alas! for these!

VII.

" A loving old couple, and tho' somewhat poor,
   " Their children had leisure to play;
" And the piper, and stranger, and beggar were
     sure
   " To bless them in going away;
" But the typhus came, and the agent too—
" Ah! need I name the worst of the two?

VIII.

" Their cot was unroofed, yet they strove to hide
   " In its walls till the fever was passed;
" Their crime was found out, and the cold ditch side
   " Was their hospital at last:

" Slowly they went to poor-house and grave,
" But the LORD *they* bent to, their *souls* will save.

IX.

" And thro' many a field you passed, and will
    pass,
    " In his lordling's ' cleared ' demesne,
" Where households as happy were once—but,
    alas!
    " They, too, are scattered or slain."
Then he pressed my hand, and he went away :
I could not stand, so I knelt to pray :

X.

"God of justice !" I sighed, "send your spirit
    down
    " On these lords so cruel and proud,
" And soften their hearts, and relax their frown,
    " *Or else*," I cried aloud—
" Vouchsafe thy strength to the peasant's hand
" To drive them at length from off the land !"*

* The scene is a mere actual landscape which I saw.

WILLIAM TELL AND THE GENIUS OF SWITZERLAND.*

I.

TELL.—You have no fears,
    My native land !
    Then dry your tears,
      And draw your brand.
A million made a vow
To free you.—Wherefore, now,
    Tears again, my native land ?

II.

GENIUS.—I weep not from doubt,
    I weep not for dread ;
    There's strength in your shout,
      And trust in your tread.
I weep, for I look for the coming dead,
    Who for Liberty's cause shall die ;
And I hear a wail from the widow's bed
    Come mixed with our triumph-cry.
Though dire my woes, yet how can I
Be calm when I know such suffering's nigh ?

---

* Just before the insurrection which expelled the Austrians, Tell and some of his brother conspirators spent a night on the shore of the Underwald Lake, consulting for liberty; and while they were thus engaged, the genius of Switzerland appeared to them, and she was armed, but weeping. "Why weep you, mother?" said Tell; and she answered: "I see dead patriots, and hear their orphans wailing." And he said again to her: "The tyrant kills us with his prisons and taxes, and poisons our air with his presence; war-death is better." And she said: "It is better." And the cloud passed from her brow, and she gave him a spear, and bade him conquer.

III.

Tell.—Death comes to all,
My native land !
Weep not their fall—
A glorious band !
Famine and slavery
Slaughter more cruelly
Than Battle's blood-covered hand !

IV.

Genius.—Yes, and all glory
Shall honour their grave,
With shrine, song, and story,
Denied to the slave.
Thus pride shall so mingle with sorrow,
Their wives half their weeping will stay ;
And their sons long to tempt on the morrow
The death they encounter to-day.
Then away, sons, to battle away !
Draw the sword, lift the flag, and away !

THE EXILE.

PARAPHRASED FROM THE FRENCH.

I.

I've passed through the nations unheeded, unknown ;
Though all looked upon me, none called me their
own.
I shared not their laughter—they cared not my moan—
For, ah ! the poor exile is always alone.

II.

At eve, when the smoke from some cottage uprose,
How happy I've thought, at the weary day's close,
With his dearest around, must the peasant repose ;
  But, ah ! the poor exile is always alone.

III.

Where hasten those clouds ? to the land or the sea—
Driven on by the tempest, poor exiles, like me ?
What matter to either where either shall flee ?
  For, ah ! the poor exile is always alone.

IV.

Those trees they are beauteous—those flowers they
  are fair ;
But no trees and no flowers of my country are there.
They speak not unto me—they heed not my care ;
  For, ah ! the poor exile is always alone.

V.

That brook murmurs softly its way through the plain ;
But the brooks of my childhood had not the same
  strain,
It reminds me of nothing—it murmurs in vain ;
  For, ah ! the poor exile is always alone.

VI.

Sweet are those songs, but their sweetness or sorrow
No charm from the songs of my infancy borrow,
I hear them to-day and forget them to-morrow ;
  For, ah ! the poor exile is always alone.

VII.

They've asked me, " Why weep you ?" I've told them
     my woe—
They listed my words, as the rocks feel the snow.
No sympathy bound us ; how could their tears flow ?
     For, sure the poor exile is always alone.

VIII.

When soft on their chosen the young maidens smile,
Like the dawn of the morn on Erin's dear isle,
With no love-smile to cheer me, I look on the while ;
     For, ah ! the poor exile is always alone.

IX.

Like boughs round the tree are those babes round
     their mother,
And these friends, like its roots, clasp and grow to
     each other ;
But, none call me child, and none call me brother :
     For, ah ! the poor exile is ever alone.

X.

Wives never clasp, and friends never smile,
Mother's ne'er fondle, nor maidens beguile ;
And happiness dwells not, except in our isle,—
     And so the poor exile is always alone.

XI.

Poor exile, cease grieving, for all are like you—
Weeping the banished, the lovely, and true.
Our country is Heaven—'twill welcome you, too ;
     And cherish the exile, no longer alone !

MY HOME.

A DREAM.

I HAVE dreamt of a home—a happy home—
The ficklest from it would not care to roam :
'Twas a cottage home on native ground,
Where all things glorious clustered round—
For highland glen and lowland plain
Met within that small demesne.

In sight is a tarn, with cliffs of fear,
Where the eagle defies the mountaineer,
And the cataract leaps in mad career,
And through oak and holly roam the deer.
On its brink is a ruined castle stern,—
The mountains are crowned with *rath* and *carn*,
Robed with heather, and bossed with stone,
And belted with a pine wood lone.

Thro' that mighty gap in the mountain chain,
Oft,'like rivers after rain,
Poured our clans on the conquered plain.
And there, upon their harrassed rear,
Oft pressed the Norman's bloody spear ;
Men call it " the pass of the leaping deer."

Wild is the region, yet gentle the spot—
As you look on the roses, the rocks are forgot ;
For garden gay, and primrose lawn
Peep through the rocks, as thro' night comes dawn.

And see, by that burn the children play ;
In that valley the village maidens stray,
Listing the thrush and the robin's lay,
Listing the burn sigh back to the breeze,
And hoping—guess whom ? 'mong the thorn trees.
Not yet, dear girls—on the uplands green
Shepherds and flocks may still be seen.

Freemen's toils, with fruit and grain,
The valley fill, and clothe the plain ;
There's the health which labour yields—
Labour tilling its own fields.
Freed at length from stranger lord—
From his frown, or his reward—
Each the owner of his land,
Plenty springs beneath his hand.

Meet these men on land or sea—
Meet them in council, war, or glee ;
Voice, glance, and mien, bespeak them free.
Welcome greets you at their hearth ;
Reverend they to age and worth ;
Yet prone to jest and full of mirth.
Fond of song, and dance, and crowd*—
Of harp, and pipe, and laughter loud ;
Their lay of love is low and bland,
Their wail for death is wild and grand ;
Awful and lovely their song of flame,
When they clash the chords in the country's name.

* Correctly *cruit*, the Irish name for the violin.

They seek no courts, and own no sway,
Save the counsels of their elders grey ;
For holy love, and homely faith,
Rule their hearts in life and death.
Yet their rifles would flash, and their sabres smite,
And their pike-staffs redden in the fight,
And young and old be swept away,
Ere the stranger in their land should sway.

But the setting sun, ere he sink in the sea,
Flushes and flashes o'er crag and tree,
Kisses the clouds with crimson sheen,
And sheets with gold the ocean's green.
Where the stately frigate lies in the bay,
The friendly fleet of the Frenchmen lay.
Yonder creek and yonder shore
Echoed then the battle's roar ;

Where, on slope after slope, the west sun shines,
After the fight lay our conquering lines.
The triumph, though great, had cost us dear ;
And the wounded and dead were lying near—
When the setting sun on our bivouac proud,
Sudden burst through a riven cloud,
An answering shout broke from our men—
Wounds and toils were forgotten then,
And dying men were heard to pray
The light would last till they passed away—
They wished to die on our triumph day.
We honoured the omen, and thought on times gone
And from chief to chief the word was passed on,
The " harp on the green " our land flag should be,
And the sun through clouds bursting, our flag at sea :

The green borne harp o'er yon battery gleams,
From the frigate's topgallant the "sunburst" streams.

In that far-off isle a sainted sage
Built a lowly hermitage,
Where ages gone made pilgrimage.
Over his grave with what weird delight,
The grey trees swim in the flooding light ;
How a halo clasps their solemn head,
Like heaven's breath on the rising dead.

Longing and languid as prisoned bird,
With a powerless dream my heart is stirred.
And I pant to pierce beyond the tomb,
And see the light or share the gloom.
But vainly for such power we pray,
God wills—enough—let man obey.

Two thousand years, 'mid sun and storm,
That tall tower has lifted its mystic form.
The yew-tree shadowing the aisle,
'Twixt airy arch and mouldering pile,
And nigh the hamlet that chapel fair
Shew religion has dwelt, and is dwelling there.

While the Druid's *crom-leac* up the vale
Tells how rites may change, and creeds may fail
Creeds may perish, and rites may fall,
But that hamlet worships the God of all.

In the land of the pious, free, and brave,
Was the happy home that sweet dream gave.
But the mirth, and beauty, and love that dwell
Within that home—I may not tell.

MY GRAVE.

SHALL they bury me in the deep,
Where wind-forgetting waters sleep ?
Shall they dig a grave for me,
Under the green-wood tree ?
Or on the wild heath,
Where the wilder breath
Of the storm doth blow ?
Oh, no ! oh, no !

Shall they bury me in the Palace Tombs,
Or under the shade of Cathedral domes ?
Sweet 'twere to lie on Italy's shore ;
Yet not there—nor in Greece, though I love it
　　more.
In the wolf or the vulture my grave shall I
　　find ?
Shall my ashes career on the world-seeing wind ?
Shall they fling my corpse in the battle mound,
Where coffinless thousands lie under the
　　ground ?
Just as they fall they are buried so—
Oh, no ! oh, no!　　　　　　　.

No ! on an Irish green hill-side,
On an opening lawn—but not too wide ;
For I love the drip of the wetted trees—
I love not the gales, but a gentle breeze,
To freshen the turf—put no tombstone there,
But green sods decked with daisies fair ;
Nor sods too deep, but so that the dew,

The matted grass-roots may trickle through.
Be my epitaph writ on my country's mind,
"HE SERVED HIS COUNTRY, AND LOVED HIS
      KIND."

Oh! 'twere merry unto the grave to go,
If one were sure to be buried so.

ᵃΟυ γὰρ φιλεῖ θεός γ᾽, αποθνήσκει νέος.

APPENDIX.

APPENDIX.

Deep sunk in that bed is the sword of Monro,
Since, twixt it and Oonagh, he met Owen Roe,

Poems, page 35.

The Blackwater in Ulster is especially remarkable as the scene of the two most memorable victories obtained by the Irish over the English power for several centuries past. The particulars of these battles are so little known, that it is hoped the following accounts of them, taken from the best accessible sources, will be acceptable to the reader. The first is from the pen of MR. DAVIS.

THE BATTLE OF BENBURB.

5TH JUNE, 1646.

The battle of Benburb was fought upon the slopes of ground, now called the Thistle Hill, from being the property of the Thistles, a family of Scotch farmers, now represented by a fine old man of over eighty years. This ground is two and a quarter miles in a right line, or three by the road, from the church of Benburb and

O

about six below Caledon, in the county Tyrone; in the angle between the Blackwater and the Oonagh, on the Benburb side of the latter, and close to Battleford Bridge. We are thus particular in marking the exact place, because of the blunders of many writers on it.

Major General Robert Monro landed with several thousand Scots at Carrickfergus, in the middle of April, 1642, and on the 28th and 29th was joined by Lord Conway and Colonel Chichester, &c., with 1800 foot, five troops of horse, and two of dragoons. Early in May, a junction was effected between Monro and Tichborne, and an army of 12,000 foot, and between 1,000 and 2,000 horse, was made up. Yet, with this vast force, Monro achieved nothing but plunder, unless the treacherous seizure of Lord Antrim be an exception. Thus was the spring of 1642 wasted. Yet, so overwhelming was Monro's force, that the Irish chiefs were thinking of giving up the war, when, on the 13th of July, OWEN ROE MAC-ART O'NEILL landed at Doe Castle, county Donegal, and received the command.

Owen Roe was born in Ulster, and at an early age entered the Spanish—the imperial service—influenced, doubtless, by the same motives that led Marshal Mac Donald into the French—that "the gates of promotion were closed at home." Owen, from his great connexions and greater abilities, rose rapidly, and held a high post in Catalonia. We have heard, through Dr. Gartland, the worthy head of the Salamanca College, that Eugenio Rufo is still remembered there. He held Arras in 1640 against the French, and (says Carte) "surrendered it at last upon honourable terms, yet his conduct in the defence was such as gave him great reputation, and procured him extraordinary respect even from the enemy."

Owen was sent for at the first outbreak in 1641, but it was not till the latter end of June, 1642, that he embarked from Dunkirk, with many of the officers and men of his own regiment, and supplies of arms. He sailed round the north of Scotland to Donegal, while another frigate brought similar succours to Wexford, under Henry O'Neill and Richard O'Farrell. Owen was immediately conducted to Charlemont, and invested with the command of Ulster.

Immediately on Owen's landing, Lesley, Earl of Leven, and General of the Scotch troops, wrote to him, saying, "he was sorry a man of his reputation and experience abroad, should come to Ireland for the maintaining of so bad a cause;" and advising his return! O'Neill replied, "he had more reason to come to relieve the deplorable state of his country, than Lesley had to march at the head of an army into England against his king, at a time when they (the Scots) were already masters of all Scotland. No contrast could be greater or better put. Lord Leven immediately embarked for Scotland, telling Monro, whom he left in command, "that he would certainly be ousted, if O'Neill once got an army together." And so it turned out. Owen sustained himself for four years against Monro on one side and Ormond on the other—harrassed by the demands of the other provincial generals, and distressed for want of provisions—defying Monro by any means to compel him to fight a battle until he was ready for it. But at length, having his troops in fine fighting order, he fought and won the greatest battle fought in Ireland since the "Yellow Ford." But we must tell how this came about.

Throughout 1642, and in the summer of 1643, Monro made two attempts to beat up O'Neill's quarters ; and though the Irish General had not *one tenth* of Monro's force, he compelled him to retire with loss into Antrim and Down. Assailed by Stewart's army on the Donegal side, Owen Roe retreated into Longford and Leitrim, hoping in the rugged districts to nurse up an army which would enable him to meet Monro in the field.

By the autumn of 1643, after having suffered many trifling losses, he had got together a militia army of 3,000 men, and the cessation having been concluded, he marched into Meath, joined Sir James Dillon, and reduced the entire district. In 1644, Monro's army amounting to 13,000 men,—O'Neill, after having for a short time occupied great part of Ulster, again returned to North Leinster. Here he was joined by Lord Castlehaven with 6,000 men ; but except trifling skirmishes, no engagement took place, and Castlehaven returned, disgusted with a war, which he had not patience to value, nor profundity to practise. 1645 passed over in similar skirmishes, in which the country suffered terribly from the plundering of Monro's army.

The leaders under Owen Roe were, Sir Phelim O'Neill, and his brother Turlough ; Con, Cormac, Hugh, and Brian O'Neill ; and the following chieftains with their clans :—Bernard Mac Mahon, the son of Hugh, chief of Monaghan, and Baron of Dartry ; Colonel Mac Mahon, Colonel Patrick Mac Neney (who was married to Helen, sister of Bernard Mac Mahon); Colonel Richard O'Ferrall of Longford; Roger Maguire of Fermanagh; Colonel Philip O'Reilly of Ballynacargy castle in the county of Cavan (who was married to Rose O'Neill, the sister of Owen Roe); and the valiant Maolmora O'Reilly (kinsman to Philip), who from his great strength and determined bravery, was called Miles the Slasher. The O'Reillys brought 200 chosen men of their own name, and of the Mac Bradys, Mac Cabes, Mac Gowans, Fitzpatricks, and Fitzsimons, from Cavan. Some fighting men were also brought by Mac Gauran of Templeport, and Mac Ternan of Croghan; some Connaught forces came with the O'Rorkes, Mac Dermots, O'Connors and O'Kellys; there came also some of the O'Donnells and O'Doghertys of Donegal; Manus O'Cane of Derry; Sir Constantine Magennis, county of Down; the O'Hanlons of Armagh, regal standard bearers of Ulster; and the O'Hagans of Tyrone.

Lords Blaney, Conway, and Montgomery commanded under Monro.

In the spring of 1646, Owen Roe met the nuncio at Kilkenny, and received from the council an ampler provision than heretofore; and by May he had completed his force under it to 5,000 foot and 5,00 horse. This army consisted partly of veterans trained by the four preceding campaigns, and partly of new levies, whom he rapidly brought into discipline by his organising genius, and his stern punishments.

With this force he marched into the county Armagh, and Monro, hearing of his movements, advanced against him by rapid marches, hoping to surprise him in Armagh city. Monro's forces consisted, according to all the best authorities, of 6,000 foot, 8,00 horse, and 7 field-pieces ; though some accounts raise his foot to 8,500, and he himself lowers it in his apologetic dispatch to 3,400, and states his field-pieces at 6.

Simultaneously with Monro's advance, his brother Colonel George Monro, marched from Coleraine, along the west shore of Loch Neagh, with three troops of horse ; and a junction was to have been effected between the two Monros and the Tyrconnell forces at Glasslough, a place in the county Monaghan, but only a few miles S. W. of Armagh. On the 4th of June Owen Roe marched from Glasslough to Benburb, confident, by means of the river and hilly country, that he could prevent the intended junction. Monro bivouacked the same night at Hamilton's Bawn, four miles from Armagh. Before dawn, on Friday, the 5th, Monro marched to Armagh town, burning houses, and wasting crops as he advanced. Fearful lest his brother, who had reached Dungannon, should be cut off, he marched towards Benburb, and on finding the strength of the Irish position there, advanced up the right bank of the Blackwater, hoping to tempt Owen from his ground. In the mean time a body of Irish horse, detached against George Monro, had met him near Dungannon, and checked his advance, though with some loss.

A good part of the day was thus spent, and it was two o'clock in the afternoon before Monro crossed the Blackwater at Kinaird (now Caledon), and led his army down the left bank of the river against O'Neill. This advance of Owen's to Ballykilgavin, was only to consume time and weary the enemy, for he shortly after retreated to Knocknacliagh, where he had determined to fight. It was now past four o'clock, when the enemy's foot advanced in a double line of columns. The first line consisted of five, and the second of four columns, much too close for manœuvring. The Irish front consisted of four, and the reserve of three divisions, with ample room.

O'Neill's position was defended on the right by a wet bog, and on the left by the junction of the Blackwater and the Oonagh. In his front was rough, hillocky ground, covered "with scrogs and bushes."

Lieutenant-Colonel Richard O'Farrell occupied some strong ground in advance of Owen's position, but Colonel Cunningham, with 500 musketeers, and the field-pieces, carried the pass, and O'Farrell effected his retreat with little loss, and no disorder. The field guns were pushed in advance by Monro, with most of his cavalry, but Owen kept the main body of his horse in reserve.

A good deal of skirmishing took place, and though the enemy had gained much ground, his soldiers were growing weary, it was five o'clock, and the evening sun of a clear and fiery June glared in their faces. While in this state, a body of cavalry was seen advancing from the north-west ; Monro declared them to be his brother's squadrons, and became confident of success. But a few minutes sufficed to undeceive him :—they were the detachments, under Colonels Bernard Mac Mahon and Patrick Mac Neney, returning from Dungannon, after having driven George Monro back upon his route.

The Scotch musketeers continued for some time to gain ground along the banks of the Oonagh, and threatened Owen's left, till the light cavalry of the

Irish broke in among them, sabred many, drove the rest across the stream, and returned without any loss.

The battle now became general. The Scotch cannon posted on a slope annoyed O'Neill's centre, and there seemed some danger of Monro's manœuvring to the west sufficiently to communicate with George Monro's corps. Owen, therefore, decided on a general attack, keeping only Rory Maguire's regiment as a reserve. His foot moved on in steady columns, and his horse in the spaces between the first and second charge of his masses. In vain did Monro's cavalry charge this determined infantry : it threw back from its face squadron after squadron, and kept constantly, rapidly, and evenly advancing. In vain did Lord Blaney take pike in hand, and stand in the ranks. Though exposed to the play of Monro's guns and musketry, the Irish infantry charged up hill without firing a shot, and closed with sabre and pike. They met a gallant resistance. Blaney and his men held their ground long, till the superior vivacity and freshness of the Irish clansmen bore him down.

An attempt was made with the columns of the rere line to regain the ground ; but from the confined space in which they were drawn up, the attempt to manœuvre them only produced disorder ; and just at this moment, to complete their ruin, O'Neill's cavalry, wheeling by the flanks of his columns, charged the Scotch cavalry, and drove them pell-mell upon the shaken and confused infantry. A total route followed. Monro, Lord Conway, Captain Burke, and forty of the horsemen escaped across the Blackwater, but most of the foot were cut to peices, or drowned in the river. 3,423 of the enemy were found on the battle-field, and Lord

Montgomery, with 21 officers and 150 men were taken prisoners. O'Neill lost 70 killed (including Colonel Manus Mac Neill and Garve O'Donnell), and 200 wounded (including Lt.-Col. O'Farrell and Phelim Mac Tuohill O'Neill). He took all the Scots artillery, twenty stand of colours, and all the arms, save those of Sir James Montgomery, whose regiment, being on Monro's extreme right, effected its retreat in some order. 1,500 draught horses and two months' provisions were also taken, but, unfortunately, Monro's ammunition blew up shortly after the battle was won. Monro fled without coat or wig to Lisburn. Moving from thence he commanded every household to furnish two musketeers; he wrote an apologetic and deceptious dispatch to the Irish committee in London, burnt Dundrum, and deserted most of Down. But all his efforts would have been in vain; for O'Neill, having increased his army, by Scotch deserters and fresh levies, to 10,000 foot and 21 troops of horse, was in the very act of breaking in on him, with a certainty of expelling the last invader from Ulster, when the fatal command of the Nuncio reached Owen at Tanderagee, ordering him to march southward to support that factious ecclesiastic against the peace. O'Neill, in an unhappy hour, obeyed the Nuncio, abandoned the fruits of his splendid victory, and marched to Kilkenny.

II

And Charlemont's cannon
Slew many a man on
    These meadows below.

Poems, page 35.

The following passage will sufficiently explain this allusion :—

"Early in June (1602) Lord Mountjoy marched by Dundalk to Armagh, and from thence, without interruption, to the banks of the Blackwater, about five miles to the eastward of Portmore, and nearer to Lough Neagh. He sent Sir Richard Moryson to the north bank of the river, commenced the building of a bridge at that point, and a castle, which he named Charlemont, from his own christian name, and stationed a garrison of one hundred and fifty men there, under the command of Captain Toby Caulfield—the founder of a noble family, which has held that spot from that day to this ; but which afterwards (as is usual with settlers in Ireland) became more Irish than many of the Irish themselves."

Mitchel's Life of Aodh O'Neill, p. 219.

III

And yonder Red Hugh
Marshal Bagenal o'erthrew
On Beal-an-atha-buidhe.
Poems, page 35.

THE BATTLE OF BEAL-AN-ATHA-BUIDHE.

10TH AUGUST, 1595.

"The tenth morning of August rose bright and serene upon the towers of Armagh and the silver waters of Avonmore. Before day dawned, the English army left the city in three divisions, and at sun-rise they were winding through the hills and woods behind the spot where now stands the little church of Grange. The sun was glancing on the corslets and spears of their glittering cavalry; their banners waved proudly, and their bugles rung clear in the morning air; when, suddenly, from the thickets on both sides of their path, a deadly volley of musketry swept through the foremost ranks. O'Neill had stationed here five hundred light-armed troops to guard the defiles; and in the shelter of thick groves of fir-trees they had silently waited for the enemy. Now they poured in their shot, volley after volley, and killed great numbers of the English; but the first division, led by Bagnal in person, after some hard fighting, carried the pass, dislodged the marks-men from their position, and drove them backwards into the plain. The centre division under Cosby and Wingfield, and the rear-guard led by Cuin and Billing, supported in flank by the cavalry under Brooke, Montacute and Fleming, now pushed forward, speedily cleared the difficult country, and formed in the open ground in front of the Irish lines. 'It was not quite safe,' says an Irish chronicler, (in admiration of Bagnal's disposition of his forces) 'to attack the nest of griffins and den of lions in which were placed the soldiers of London.' Bagnal, at the head of his first division, and aided by a body of cavalry, charged the Irish light-armed troops up to the very entrenchments, in front of which O'Neill's foresight had prepared some pits, covered over with wattles and grass; and many of the English cavalry rushing impetuously forward, rolled headlong, both men and horses, into these trenches and perished. Still the Marshal's chosen troops, with loud cheers and shouts of 'St. George for merry England!' resolutely attacked the entrenchments that stretched across the pass, battered them with cannon, and in one place succeeded, though with heavy loss, in forcing back their defenders. Then first the main body of O'Neill's troops was brought into action; and with bag-pipes sounding a charge, they fell upon the English, shouting their fierce battle-cries, *Lamhdearg!* and *O'Domhnaill Abu!* O'Neill himself, at the head of a body of horse, pricked forward to seek out Bagnal amidst the throng of battle; but they never met: the marshal, who had done his devoir that day like a good soldier, was shot through the brain by some unknown marksman: the division he had led was forced back by the furious onslaught of the Irish, and put to utter rout; and, what added to their confusion, a cart of gunpowder exploded amidst the English ranks and blew many of their men to atoms. And now the cavalry of Tyrconnell and Tyrowen dashed into the plain and

bore down the remnant of Brooke's and Fleming's
horse : the columns of Wingfield and Cosby reeled before their rushing charge—while, in front, to the war-
cry of *Batailla Abu !* the swords and the axes of the
heavy-armed galloglasses were raging amongst the
Saxon ranks. By this time the cannon were all taken;
the cries of 'St. George' had failed, or turned into
death-shrieks ; and once more, England's royal standard sunk beneath the Red Hand of Tyr-owen.

"The last who resisted was the traitor O'Reilly:
twice he tried to rally the flying squadrons, but was
slain in the attempt ; and at last the whole of that
fine army was utterly routed, and fled pell-mell
towards Armagh, with the Irish hanging fiercely on
their rear. Amidst the woods and marshes all con-
nexion and order were speedily lost ; and as O'Donnell's chronicler has it, they were ' pursued in couples,
in threes, in scores, in thirties, and in hundreds,' and
so cut down in detail by their avenging pursuers. In
one spot especially the carnage was terrible, and the
country people yet point out the lane where that
hideous rout passed by, and call it to this day the
' Bloody Loaning.' Two thousand five hundred English were slain in the battle and flight, including
twenty three superior officers, besides lieutenants and
ensigns. Twelve thousand gold pieces, thirty-four
standards, all the musical instruments and cannon,
with a long train of provision waggons, were a rich
spoil for the Irish army. The confederates had only
two hundred slain and six hundred wounded."

Michel's Life of Aodh O'Neill, pp. 141—144.

IV.

CYMRIC RULE AND CYMRIC RULERS.

Poems, page 41.

This poem has less title than any other in Part I. to be ranked among National (*i. e.* either in subject, or by aim or allusion, Irish) Ballads and Songs, unless the affinity of the Cymric with the Irish Celts, and the fact that the author himself was of Welsh extraction by the father's side, be considered a sufficient justification.

Mr. Davis was very fond of the air—" The March of the Men of Harlech," to which this poem is set. To evince his strong partiality for, and sympathy with, the Welsh people, it is enough to quote the following passages from one of his political essays—

" We just now opened *M'Culloch's Geographical Dictionary* to ascertain some Welsh statistics, and found at the name " Wales" a reference to " England and Wales," and at the latter title nothing distinct on the Principality ; and what was there, was rather inferior to the information on Cumberland, or most English counties.

" 'And has time, then,' we said, ' mouldered away that obstinate and fiery tribe of Celts which baffled the Plantagenets, which so often trod upon the breast-plates of the Norman, which sometimes bent in the summer, but ever rose when the fierce elements of winter came to aid the native ?   Has that race passed away which stood under Llewellyn, and rallied under Owen Glendower, and gave the Dragon flag and

Tudor kings to England? Is the prophesy of twelve hundred years false—are the people and tongue passed away?'

"No! spite of the massacre of bards, and the burning of records—spite of political extinction, there is a million of these Kymrys in Wales and its marches ; and nine out of ten of these speak their old tongue, follow their old customs, sing the songs which the sleepers upon Snowden made, have their religious rites in Kymric, and hate the Logrian as much as ever their fathers did. * * * * * *

" Twenty-nine Welsh members could do much if united, more especially if they would co-operate with the Irish and Scotch members in demanding their share of the imperial expenditure ; or what would be safer and better, in agitating for a local council to administer the local affairs of the Principality. A million of the Kymry, who are still apart in their mountains, who have *immense* mineral resources, and some good harbours, one (Milford) the best in Britain, and who are of our blood, nearly of our old and un-English language, have as good a right to a local senate as the 700,000 people of Greece, or the half million of Cassel or Mecklenburgh have to independence, or as each of the States of America has to a local congress. Localisation, by means of Federalism, seems the natural and best resource of a country like Wales, to guard its purse, and language, and character, from imperial oppression, and its soil·from foreign invasion. As powers run, it is not like Ireland, quite able, if free, to hold her own ; but it has importance enough to entitle it to a local congress for its local affairs."

P

V.

THE IRISH HURRAH.

Poems, page 46.

The second stanza of this poem, as it appears in the text, was omitted by the author in a later copy; it would seem, with a view of adapting it better to the air to which it is set.

VI.

A CHRISTMAS SCENE.

Poems, page 85.

The first sketch of this poem differs a good deal from that in the text. It is so pleasing that it is given here as originally published. It was then entitled :—

A CHRISTMAS CAROL.

I.

THE hill-blast comes howling from leaf-rifted trees,
Which late were as harp-strings to each gentle breeze;
The sportsmen have parted, the blue-stockings gone,
While we sit happy-hearted—together, alone.

II.

The glory of nature through the window has charms,
But within, gentle Kate, you're entwined in my arms;
The sportsmen may seek for snipe, woodcock and hare—
The snow is on their cheek, on mine your black hair.

III.

The painters may rave of the light and the shade,
The *blues* and the poets of lake, hill, and glade;
While the light of yonr eye, and your soft wavy form
Suit a proser like me by the hearth bright and warm.

IV.

My Kate, I'm so happy, your voice whispers soft,
And your cheek flushes wilder by kissing so oft;
Should our kiss grow less fond, or the weather serene,
Forth together we'll wander to see each loved scene.

V.

And at eve, as the sportsmen and pedants will say,
As they swallow their dinner, how they spent the day,
Your eye, roguish-smiling, to me only will say
That more sweetly than any, you and I spent the day.

VII.

THE FATE OF KING DATHI.

Poems, p. 97.

The real adventures of this warlike king, the last of
the Pagan monarchs of Ireland, and likewise the last
who extended his conquests to the continent of Europe
are, like too much of the ancient annals of this country,
obscured by the mixture of pious or romantic legends
with authentic history. An accurate account of

Dathi, and his immediate predecessors, will be found in the Addenda to Mr. O'Donovan's excellent edition of the *Tribes and Customs of the Ui-Fiachrach*, printed for the Irish Archæological Society ; from which the following passages are extracted.

"In the life-time of Niall of the Nine Hostages, Brian, his brother of the half-blood, became King of Connaught, and his second brother of the half-blood, Fiachra, the ancestor of the O'Dowds and all the Ui-Fiachrach tribes, became chief of the district extending from Carn Fearadhaigh, near Limerick, to Magh Mucroime, near Athenry. But dissensions soon arose between Brian and his brother Fiachra, and the result was that a battle was fought between them, in which the latter was defeated, and delivered as a hostage into the hands of his half-brother, Niall of the Nine Hostages. After this, however, Dathi, a very warlike youth, waged war on his uncle Brian, and challenged him to a pitched battle, at a place called Damh-cluain, not far from Knock-mea-hill, near Tuam. In this battle, in which Dathi was assisted by Crimthann, son of Enna Cennseloch, King of Leinster, Brian and his forces were routed, and pursued from the field of battle to Fulcha Domhnaill, where he was overtaken and slain by Crimthann.   *   *   *   *   *   *

"After the fall of Brian, Fiachra was set at liberty and installed King of Connaught, and enjoyed that dignity for twelve years, during which period he was general of the forces of his brother Niall. *   *   *   * According to the book of Lecan, this Fiachra had five sons, of which the most eminent were Dathi, and Amhalgaidh (*vulgo* Awley) King of Connaught, who died in the year 449. The seven sons of this Amhal-

gaidh, together with twelve thousand men, are said to
have been baptized in one day by St. Patrick, at
Forrach Mac n'Amhalgaidh, near Killala.

"On the death of his father Fiachra, Dathi became
King of Connaught, and on the death of his uncle,
Niall of the Nine Hostages, he became Monarch of
Ireland, leaving the government of Connaught to his
less warlike brother, Amhalgaidh. King Dathi,
following the example of his predecessor, Niall, not
only invaded the coasts of Gaul, but forced his way to
the very foot of the Alps, where he was killed by a
flash of lightning, leaving the throne of Ireland to be
filled by a line of Christian kings."

Tribes and Customs of the Ui-Fiachrach—Addenda,
pp. 344-6.

VIII.

ARGAN MOR

Poems, page 101.

Mr. Davis was very fond of the air for which this
poem was composed, and which suggested its name.
It is a simple air, of great antiquity, preserved in
Bunting's Third Collection, where it is No. V. of the
airs marked "very ancient." The following is Mr.
Bunting's account of it :—

"*Argan Mor.*—An Ossianic air, still sung to the
words preserved by Dr. Young, and published in the
first volume of the Transactions of the Royal Irish
Academy. The editor took down the notes from the
singing, or rather recitation, of a native of Murloch,

in the county of Antrim. This sequestered district
lies along the sea-shore, between Tor Point and Fair
Head, and is still rife with traditions, both musical and
legendary. From the neighbouring ports of Cushen-
dun and Cushendall was the principal line of com-
munication with Scotland; and, doubtless, it was by
this route that the Ossianic poems themselves found
their way into that country."—*Ancient Music of Ireland*—Preface p. 88.

IX.

THE TRUE IRISH KING.

Poems, page 103.

In an essay on Ballad History, Mr Davis refers to
this poem, as an attempt to show how the materials
and hints, scattered through antiquarian volumes,
may be brought together and presented with effect in
a poetical form. The subject is one involved in un-
usual obscurity, considering its importance in Irish
History. The chief notices of the custom have been
collected by Mr. O'Donovan in the Addenda to his
edition of the *Tribes and Customs of the Ui-Fiachrach*,
pp. 425—452, to which work the reader is referred,
who may wish to trace the *disjecta membra poematis*,
in the scattered hints and traditions of which Mr.
Davis has availed himself.

X.

O'SULLIVAN'S RETURN.

Poems, page 119.

The following description was prefixed to this ballad by the author, on its first publication : —

" This ballad is founded on an ill-remembered story of an Irish chief, returning after long absence on the Continent, and being wrecked and drowned close to his own castle.

" The scene is laid in Bantry Bay, which runs up into the county of Cork, in a north-easterly direction. A few miles from its mouth, on your left hand as you go up, lies Beare Island (about seven miles long), and between it and the mainland of Beare lies Beare Haven, one of the finest harbours in the world. Dunboy Castle, near the present Castletown, was on the main, so as to command the south-western entrance to the haven.

" Further up, along the same shore of Beare, is Adragoole, a small gulf off Bantry Bay.

" The scene of the wreck is at the south-eastern shore of Beare Island. A ship, steering from Spain, by Mizenhead for Dunboy, and caught by a southerly gale, if unable to round the point of Beare and to make the Haven, should leave herself room to run up the bay, towards Adragoole, or some other shelter."

XI.

—Dunbwy is lying lowly.

The halls where mirth and minstrelsy
Than Beara's wind rose louder,
Are flung in masses lonelily,
And black with English powder.

Poems, page 126.

The destruction of O'Sullivan's Castle of Dunboy
or Dunbwy, (correctly *Dunbaoi* or *Dunbuidhe*) is well
described by Mr. Mitchel.—*Life of Aodh O'Neill,*
p. 216.

"Mountjoy spent that spring in Munster, with the
President, reducing those fortresses which still re-
mained in the hands of the Irish, and fiercely crushing
down every vestige of the national war. Richard
Tyrrell, however, still kept the field ; and O'Sullivan
Beare held his strong castle of Dun-buidhe, which he
wrested from the Spaniards after Don Juan had
stipulated to yield it to the enemy. This castle commanded Bantry Bay, and was one of the most impor-
tant fortresses in Munster ; and therefore Carew
determined, at whatever cost, to make himself master
of it. Dun-buidhe was but a square tower, with
a court-yard and some out-works, and had but 140
men ; yet it was so strongly situated, and so bravely
defended, that it held the Lord President and an
army of four thousand men, with a great train of
artillery and some ships of war, fifteen days before

its walls. After a breach was made, the storming parties were twice driven back to their lines ; and even after the great hall of the castle was carried, the garrison, under their indomitable commander, Mac Geoghegan, held their ground in the vaults underneath for a whole day, and at last fairly beat the besiegers out of the hall. The English cannon then played furiously upon the walls ; and the President swore to bury these obstinate Irish under the ruins. Again a desperate sortie was made by forty men—they were all slain ; eight of them leaped into the sea to save themselves by swimming ; but Carew, anticipating this, had stationed Captain Harvy, 'with three boats to keepe the sea, but had the killing of them all ;' and at last, after Mac Geoghegan was mortally wounded, the remnant of the garrison laid down their arms. Mac Geoghegan lay, bleeding to death, on the floor of the vault ; yet when he saw the besiegers admitted, he raised himself up, snatched a lighted torch, and staggered to an open powder barrel—one moment, and the castle, with all it contained, would have rushed skyward in a pyramid of flame, when suddenly an English soldier seized him in his arms : he was killed on the spot, and all the rest were shortly after executed. 'The whole number of the ward,' says Carew, 'consisted of one hundred and forty-three selected men, being the best choice of all their forces, of which not one man escaped, but were either slain, executed, or buried in the ruins ; and so obstinate a defence hath not been seen within this kingdom.' Perhaps some will think that the survivors of so brave a band deserved a better fate than hanging."

XII.

LAMENT FOR OWEN ROE O'NEILL.

Poems, page 133.

This poem was issued by the author with the following explanatory sketch :—

"In 1649, the country being exhausted, Owen made a truce with Monk, Coote, and the Independents—a truce observed on both sides, though Monk was severely censured by the English Parliament for it.— (*Journals, 10th August*, 1649.) On its expiration, O'Neill concluded a treaty with Ormond, 12th October, 1649 ; and so eager was he for it, that ere it was signed, he sent over 3,000 men, under Major-General O'Farrell, to join Ormond, (which they did October 25th.) Owen himself strove with all haste to follow, to encounter Cromwell, who had marched south after the sack of Drogheda. But fate and an unscrupulous foe forbade. Poison, it is believed, had been given him either at Derry or shortly after. His constitution struggled with it for some time ; slowly and sinking he marched through Tyrone and Monaghan into Cavan, and,—anxiously looked for by Ormond, O'Farrell, and the southern corps and army,—lingered till the 6th of November (St. Leonard's feast), when he died at Clough Oughter Castle,—then the seat of Maelmorra O'Reilly, and situated on a rock in Lough Oughter, some six miles west of Cavan. He was buried, says Carte, in Cavan Abbey ; but report says his sepulchre was concealed, lest it should be violated by the English. The news of his death reached Ormond's camp when the Duke was preparing to fight Cromwell,—when Owen's genius and soldiers were most needed. All writers (even to the sceptical Dr. O'Conor, of Stowe) admit that had Owen lived, he would have saved Ireland. His gallantry, his influence, his genius, his soldiers, all combine to render it probable. The rashness with which the stout bishop, Ebher Mac Mahon, led 4,000 of Owen's veterans to death at Letterkenny, the year after ; and the way in which Ormond frittered away the strength of O'Farrell's division (though 1,200 of them slew 2,000 of Cromwell's men in the breach at Clonmel),—and the utter prostration which followed, showed Ireland how great was her loss when Owen died.

"O'Farrell, Red Hugh O'Neill, and Mac Mahon, were Ulster generals ; Audley, Lord Castlehaven, and Preston, commanded in the south and east ; the Marquis of Clanrickarde was president of Connaught."

Mr. Davis grounded his stanzas on a popular belief which not only prevailed at the time of Owen Roe's death, but subsequently became incorporated with the facts of history, that the general died by poison given him at a banquet in Derry. This treachery, however, had no just foundation. The exact circumstances connected with Owen's death were first made known to the public by the researches of the Rev. C. P. Meehan, to whom the civil history of his country is more indebted than even the ecclesiastical, and for whose labours there is one reward—a durable and glorious name. In a M.S. preserved in Trinity Col-

lege, and written by a contemporary of the great
chieftain, Father Meehan discovered the first authentic particulars connected with his decease and brought
them to light in the first number of this Series. But
in that beautiful and charming volume—one of the
most remarkable ever published—" The Flight of the
Earls," the author gratifies the most anxious curiosity
respecting the hero's fate, by reprinting, from the
original in the State Paper Office, a letter written by
the dying chieftain to the Marquis of Ormonde. As
to the nature of his disease there existed an uncertainty
with the patient and his medical attendant. He complained chiefly of pains in the knees, and it is
probable that they had their origin in some acute
rheumatic or gouty ailment. He was buried in the
Franciscan Convent, Cavan ; see *Flight of the Earls,*
p. 472.

XIII.

A RALLY FOR IRELAND.

Poems, page 135.

There is no period in Irish, or in English History,
which has been so much misrepresented, or of which
so utterly discordant opinions are still entertained, as
the Revolution of 1688—91. The English history of
that revolution has been elaborately sifted, and its
hidden causes successively dragged to light, by men of
remarkable eminence in literature and in politics. It

is sufficient to mention in England, Mr. Fox, Sir
James Mackintosh, Mr. Hallam, Dr. Lingard, and
Mr. Ward ;—in France, M. Thierry (*Historical Essays*,
No. VI.,) M. Carrel, and M. De Mazire,—and among
Irishmen, Mr. W. Wallace, (*Continuation of Mackintosh's History*,) and Mr. Torrens Mac Cullagh, (Articles
in the *North of England Magazine*, for 1842, and in
the *Dublin Magazine*, for 1843.) A minute study of
some at least of these writers—Mr. Wallace's history is,
perhaps, on the whole, the fairest and most comprehensive—is indispensable to a correct understanding
of the Irish question.

In the *Dublin Magazine*, for 1843, January to April,
Mr. Davis devoted a series of papers to a critical
examination of some of the Irish authorities, on this
subject, principally in regard to the Irish Parliament
of 1689. His aim was to vindicate the character of
that legislature, and to refute some of the most glaring
falsehoods which had hitherto, by dint of impudent
re-assertion, passed almost unquestioned by Irishmen
of every shade of political opinion. Falsehoods of a
more injurious tendency have never been current
among a people ; and the effort to expose them was
with Mr. Davis, a labour of zeal and love ; for he
knew well how much of the religious dissension
which has been and is the ruin of Ireland, took its
rise from, and stands rooted in, erroneous conceptions
of that time. To these papers the reader is referred,
who is anxious to form an accurate, and withal a
national judgment of the cardinal crisis in Irish
History.

How high the hopes of Ireland were at the com
mencement of this struggle, and how she cherished

afterwards the memories and hopes bequeathed from it, is abundantly illustrated by the Jacobite Relics in Mr. Hardiman's *Irish Minstrelsy*, and in the more lecrecent coltion by Mr. Daly.

XIV.

BALLADS AND SONGS OF THE BRIGADE.

Poems, p. 144.

So considerable a space in this volume is occupied by poems, founded on the adventures and services of the Irish Brigade, that it seemed right to include here the following sketch, written by Mr. Davis in the year 1844 :—

HISTORICAL SKETCH OF THE IRISH BRIGADE.

INTRODUCTION.

The foreign military achievements of the Irish began on their own account. They conquered and colonized Scotland, frequently overran England during and after the Roman dominion there, and more than once penetrated into Gaul. During the time of the Danish invasion, they had enough to do at home. The progress of the English conquest brought them again to

battle on foreign ground. It is a melancholy fact
that in the brigades wherewith Edward I. ravaged,
Scotland, there were numbers of Irish and Welsh.
Yet Scotland may be content; Wales and Ireland
suffered from the same baseness. The sacred heights
of Snowdon (the Parnassus of Wales) were first forced
by Gascon mountaineers, whose independence had
perished; and the Scotch did no small share of blood-
work for England here, from the time of Monro's
defeats in the seventeenth century, to the Fencible
victories over drunken peasants in 1798.

In these levies of Edward I., as in those of his
son, were numbers of native Irish. The Connaught
clans in particular seem to have served these Plantagenets.

From Edward Bruce's invasion, the English control
was so broken that the Irish clans ceased to serve
altogether, and indeed, shortly after, made many of
the Anglo-Irish pay them tribute. But the lords of
the Pale took an active and prominent part in the
wars of the Roses; and their vassals shared the
victories, the defeats, and the carnage of the time.

In the continental wars of Edward III. and
Henry V., the Norman-Irish served with much
distinction.

Henry VIII. demanded of the Irish government
2,000 men, 1,000 of whom were, if possible, to be
gunners, i. e. armed with matchlocks. The services
of these Irish during the short war in France, and
especially at the siege of Boulogne, are well known.

At the submission of Ireland in 1603, O'Sullivan
Bearra, and some others excepted from the amnesty,
took service and obtained high rank in Spain; and

after the flight of O'Neill and O'Donnell in 1607, numbers of Irish crowded into all the Continental services. We find them holding commissions in Spain, France, Austria, and Italy.

Scattered among "*Strafford's Letters*," various indications are discoverable of the estimation in which the Irish were held as soldiers in foreign services during the early part of the seventeenth century. The Spanish government in particular seems to have been extremely desirous of enlisting in Ireland, their own troops at that time being equal, if not superior, to any in the world, especially their infantry.

Nor were the Irish troops less active for the English king. Strafford had increased the Irish army. These he paid regularly, clothed well, and frequently "drew out in large bodies." He meant to oppress, but discipline is a precious thing, no matter who teaches it—a Strafford or a Wellington; and during the wars which followed 1641, some of these troops he had raised, served Ireland. In 1639, when the first row with the Scotch took place, Wentworth was able to send a garrison of 500 Irish to Carlisle, and other forces to assist Charles. And the victories of Montrose were owing to the valour and discipline of the Irish auxiliaries under Colkitto (left-handed) Alister Mac Donnell.

Many of the Irish who had lost their fortunes by the Cromwellian wars, served on the Continent.

Tyrconnell increased the Irish army, but with less judgment than Strafford. Indeed, numbers of his regiments were ill-officered mobs, and, when real work began in 1689, were disbanded as having neither arms nor discipline. His sending of the Irish troops to England hastened the Revolution by exciting jealousy, and they were too mere a handful to resist. They were forced to enter the service of German princes, especially the Prussian.

SERVICES OF THE IRISH BRIGADE.

The year before the English Revolution of 1688, William effected the league of Augsburg, and combined Spain, Italy, Holland and the empire, against France ; but, except some sieges of imperial towns, the war made no great progress till 1690. In that year France blazed out ruin on all sides. The Palatinate was overrun and devastated. The defeat of Humieres at Valcourt was overweighed by Luxemburgh's great victory over Prince Waldech at Fleurus.

But as yet, no Irish troops served north of the Alps. It was otherwise in Italy.

The Duke of Savoy having joined the Allies, Marshal Catinat entered his territories at the head of 18,000 men. Mountcashel's brigade, which landed in May and had seen service, formed one-third of this corps. Catinat, a disciple of Turenne, relied on his infantry ; nor did he err in this instance. On the 8th of August, 1690, he met the Duke of Savoy and Prince Eugene at Staffardo, near Salucco. The battle began by a feigned attack on the Allies' right wing. The real attack was made by ten battalions of infantry, who crossed some marshes heretofore deemed impassible, turned the left wing, commanded by Prince Eugene, drove it in on the centre, and totally routed the enemy. The Irish troops ("bog-trotters," the *Times* calls us now) proved that

Q

there are more qualities in a soldier than the light step and hardy frame which the Irish bog gives to its inhabitants.

But the gallant Mountcashel received a wound, of which he died soon after at Bareges.

This same brigade continued to serve under Catinat throughout the Italian campaigns of '91, '92, and '93.

The principal action of this last year was at Marsiglia on the 4th October. It was not materially different in tactic from Staffardo. Catinat cannonaded the Allies from a height, made a feigned attack in the centre, while his right wing lapped round Savoy's left, tumbled it in, and routed the army with a loss of 8,000, including Duke Schomberg, son to him who died at the Boyne. On this day, too, the Munster soldiers had their full share of the laurels.

They continued to serve during the whole of this war against Savoy; and when in 1698, the Duke changed sides, and, uniting his forces with Catinat's, laid siege to Valenza in North Italy, the Irish distinguished themselves again. No less than six Irish regiments were at the siege.

While these campaigns were going on in Italy, the garrison of Limerick landed in France, and the second Irish Brigade was formed.

The Flanders campaign of '91 hardly went beyond skirmishes.

Louis opened 1692 by besieging Namur at the head of 120,000 men, including the bulk of the Irish Brigade. Luxemburgh was the actual commander, and Vauban the engineer. Namur, one of the greatest fortresses of Flanders, was defended by Cœhorn, the all but equal of Vauban; and William advanced to its relief at the head of 100,000 men,—illustrious players of that fearful game. But French and Irish valour, pioneered by Vauban and manœuvred by Luxemburgh, prevailed. In seven days Namur was taken, and shortly after the citadel surrendered, though within shot of William's camp.

Louis returned to Versailles, and Luxemburgh continued his progress.

On the 24th of July, 1692, William attempted to steal a victory from the Marshal who had so repeatedly beaten him. Having forced a spy to persuade Luxemburgh that the Allies meant only to forage, he made an attack on the French camp, then placed between Steenkirk and Enghien. Wirtemburg and Mackay had actually penetrated the French camp ere Luxemburgh mounted his horse. But, so rapid were his movements, so skilfully did he divide the Allies and crush Wirtemburgh ere Count Solmes could help him, that the enemy was driven off with the loss of 3,000 men, and many colours and cannon.

Sarsfield, who commanded the Brigade that day, was publicly thanked for his conduct. In March, 1693, he was made a Mareschal de Camp.

But his proud career was drawing to a close. He was slain on the 29th July, 1693, at Landen, heading his countrymen in the van of victory, King William flying. He could not have died better. His last thoughts were for his country. As he lay on the field unhelmed and dying, he put his hand to his breast. When he took it away, it was full of his best blood. Looking at it sadly with an eye in which victory shone a moment before, he said faintly, " Oh ! that this were

Q

for Ireland." He said no more; and history records no
nobler saying, nor any more becoming death.*

It is needless to follow out the details of the Italian
and Flanders campaigns. Suffice that bodies of the
Irish troops served in each of the great armies, and
maintained their position in the French ranks during
years of hard and incessant war.

James II. died at St. Germain's on the 16th September, 1701, and was buried in the church of the English
Benedictines in Paris. But his death did not affect
the Brigade. Louis immediately acknowledged his
son, James III., and the Brigade, upon which the
king's hopes of restoration lay, was continued.

In 1701, Sheldon's cavalry, then serving under
Catinat in Italy, had an engagement with the cavalry
corps under the famous Count Merci, and handled
them so roughly that Sheldon was made a lieutenant-
general of France, and the supernumeraries of his
corps were put on full pay.

In January, 1702, occurred the famous rescue of
Cremona. Villeroy succeeded Catinat in August,
1701, and having with his usual rashness attacked
Eugene's camp at Chiari, he was defeated. Both
parties retired early to winter quarters, Eugene encamping so as to blockade Mantua. While thus
placed, he opened an intrigue with one Cassoli, a
priest of Cremona, where Villeroy had his head quarters. An old aqueduct passed under Cassoli's house,
and he had it cleared of mud and weeds by the

* According to Mr. O'Connor, (*Military History of the Irish Nation*,
p. 223,) "there was no Irish corps in the army of Luxemburgh, and
Sarsfield fell leading on a charge of Strangers." But this only makes his
death, and the regrets which accompanied it, the more affecting. ED.

authorities, under pretence that his house was injured from want of drainage. Having opened this way, he got several of Eugene's grenadiers into the town disguised, and now at the end of January all was ready.

Cremona lies on the left bank of the river Po.* It was then five miles round, and guarded by a strong castle and by an *enceinte*, or continued fortification all round it, pierced by five gates. One of these gates led almost directly to the bridge over the Po. This bridge was fortified by a redoubt.

Eugene's design was to surprise the town at night. He meant to penetrate on two sides, south and north. Prince Charles of Vaudemont crossed the Po at Firenzola, and marching up the right bank with 2,500 foot and 500 horse, was to assault the bridge and gate of the Po, as soon as Eugene had entered on the north. As this northern attack was more complicated, and as it succeeded, it may be best described in the narrative of events.

On the 31st of January Eugene crossed the Oglio at Ustiano, and approached the north of the town. Marshal Villeroy had that night returned from a war council at Milan.

At three o'clock in the morning of the 1st of February, the allies closed in on the town in the following order :—1,100 men under Count Kufstein entered by the aqueduct ; 300 men were led to the gate of St. Margaret's, which had been walled up, and immediately commenced removing the wall from it ; mean-

---

* In talking of right or left banks of rivers, you are supposed to be looking down the stream. Thus, Connaught is on the right bank of the Shannon ; Leinster and Munster on its left bank.

time, the other troops under Kufstein pushed on and secured the ramparts to some distance, and as soon as the gate was cleared, a vanguard of horse under Count Merci dashed through the town. Eugene, Staremberg, and Prince Commerci followed with 7,000 horse and foot. Patrols of cavalry rode the streets; Staremberg seized the great square; the barracks of four regiments were surrounded, and the men cut down as they appeared.

Marshal Villeroy hearing the tumult, hastily burned his papers and rode out attended only by a page. He was quickly snapped up by a party of Eugene's cavalry commanded by an Irishman named Macdonnell. Villeroy seeing himself in the hands of a soldier of fortune, hoped to escape by bribery. He made offer after offer. A thousand pistoles and a regiment of horse were refused by this poor Irish captain; and Villeroy rode out of the town with his captor.

The Marquis of Mongon, General Crenant, and other officers shared the same fate, and Eugene assembled the town council to take an oath of allegiance, and supply him with 14,000 rations. All seemed lost.

All was not lost. The Po gate was held by 35 Irishmen, and to Merci's charge and shout they answered with a fire that forced their assailant to pass on to the rampart, where he seized a battery. This unexpected and almost rash resistance was the very turning point of the attack. Had Merci got this gate, he had only to ride on and open the bridge to Prince Vaudemont. The entry of 3,000 men more, and on that side, would have soon ended the contest.

Not far from this same gate of the Po were the

quarters of two Irish regiments, Dillon (one of
Mountcashel's old brigade and Burke (the Athlone
regiment.. Dillon's regiment was, in Colonel Lacy's
absence, commanded by Major Mahony. He had
ordered his regiment to assemble for exercise at day-
break, and lay down. He was awoke by the noise
of the Imperial Cuirassiers passing his lodgings. He
jumped up, and finding how things were, got off to
the two corps, and found them turning out in their
shirts to check the Imperialists, who swarmed round
their quarters.

He had just got his men together when General
D'Arenes came up, put himself at the head of these
regiments, who had nothing but their muskets, shirts
and cartouches about them. He instantly led them
against Merci's force, and after a sharp struggle, drove
them from the ramparts, killing large numbers, and
taking many prisoners, amongst others Macdonnell,
who returned to fight after securing Villeroy.

In the mean time E tragne's regiment had made a
post of a few houses in the great square : Count Revel
had given the word "French to the ramparts," and
retook All-Saints' Gate, while M. Praslin made head
against the Imperial Cavalry patroles. But when
Revel attempted to push further round the ramparts
and regain St. Margaret's Gate he was repulsed with
heavy loss, and D'Arenes, who seems to have been
everywhere, was wounded.

It was now ten o'clock in the day, and Mahony
had received orders to fight his way from the Po to
the Mantua Gate, leaving a detachment to guard the
rampart from which he had driven Merci. He pushed
on, driving the enemies' infantry before him, but

suffering much from their fire, when Baron Freiberg at the head of a regiment of Imperial Cuirassiers, burst into Dillon's regiment. For a while their case seemed desperate; but almost naked as they were, they grappled with their foes. The linen shirt and steel cuirass—the naked footmen and the harnessed cavalier met, and the conflict was desperate and doubtful. Just at this moment Mahony grasped the bridle of Freiberg's horse, and bid him ask quarter. "No quarter to-day," said Freiberg, dashing his spurs into his horse; he was instantly shot. The Cuirassiers saw and paused; the Irish shouted and slashed at them. The volley came better and the sabres wavered. Few of the Cuirassiers lived to fly; but all who survived did fly: and there stood these glorious fellows in the wintry streets, bloody, triumphant, half-naked. Bourke lost seven officers and forty-two soldiers killed, and nine officers and fifty soldiers wounded; Dillon had one officer and forty-nine soldiers killed, and twelve officers and seventy-nine soldiers wounded.

But what matter for death or wounds! Cremona is saved. Eugene waited long for Vaudemont, but the French, guarded from Merci's attack by the Irish picquet of 35, had ample time to evacuate the redoubt and ruin the bridge of boats.

On hearing of Freiberg's death, Eugene made an effort to keep the town by frightening the council. On hearing of the destruction of the bridge, he despaired, and effected his retreat with consummate skill, retaining Villeroy and 100 other officers prisoners.

Europe rang with applause. Mr. Forman mentions what we think a very doubtful saying of King Wil-

liam's about this event. There is no such question as
to King Louis. He sent his public and formal thanks
to them, and raised their pay forthwith. We would
not like to meet the Irishman who, knowing these
facts, would pass the north of Italy, and not track
the steps of the Irish regiments through the streets
and gates and ramparts of Cremona.

In the campaigns of 1703, the Irish distinguished
themselves under Vendome in Italy, at Vittoria,
Luzzara, Cassano, and Calcinato, and still more on
the Rhine. When Villars won the battle of Freidlin-
gen, the Irish had their share of the glory. At Spires,
when Tallard defeated the Germans, they had more.
Tallard had surprised the enemy, but their commander, the Prince of Hesse, rallied his men, and al-
though he had three horses shot under him, he repelled
the attack and was getting his troops well into hand.
At this crisis Nugent's regiment of horse was ordered
to charge a corps of German cuirassiers. They did
so effectually. The German cavalry was cut up; the
French infantry thus covered returned to their work,
and Hesse was finally defeated with immense loss.

And now the fortunes of France began to waver,
but the valour of the Brigade did not change.

It is impossible in our space to do more than glance
at the battles in which they won fame amid general
defeat.

At the battle of Hochstet or Blenheim in 1704,
Marshal Tallard was defeated and taken prisoner by
Marlborough and Eugene. The French and Bava-
rians lost 10,000 killed, 13,000 prisoners, and 90 pieces
of cannon. Yet amid this monstrous disaster, Clare's
dragoons were victorious over a portion of Eugene's

famous cavalry, and took two standards. And in the battle of Ramillies in 1706, where Villeroy was utterly routed, Clare's dragoons attempted to cover the wreck of the retreating French, broke through an English regiment, and followed them into the thronging van of the Allies. Mr. Forman states that they were generously assisted out of this predicament by an Italian regiment, and succeeded in carrying off the English colours they had taken.

At the sad days of Oudenarde and Malplaquet, some of them were also present ; but to the victories which brightened this time, so dark to France, the Brigade contributed materially. At the battle of Almanza (13th March, 1707), several Irish regiments served under Berwick. In the early part of the day the Portuguese and Spanish auxiliaries of England were broken, but the English and Dutch fought successfully for a long time ; nor was it till repeatedly charged by the elite of Berwick's army, including the Irish, that they were forced to retreat. 3,000 killed, 10,000 prisoners, and 120 standards attested the magnitude of the victory. It put King Philip on the throne of Spain. In the siege of Barcelona, Dillon's regiment fought with great effect. In their ranks was a boy of twelve years old ; he was the son of a Galway gentleman, Mr. Lally or O'Lally of Tulloch na Daly, and his uncle had sat in James's parliament of 1689. This boy, so early trained, was afterwards the famous Count Lally de Tollendal, whose services in every part of the globe make his execution a stain upon the honour as well as upon the justice of Louis XVI. And when Villars swept off the whole of Albemarle's battalions at Denain, in 1712, the Irish were in his van.

The treaty of Utrecht and the dismissal of Marlborough put an end to the war in Flanders, but still many of the Irish continued to serve in Italy and Germany, and thus fought at Parma, Guastalla, and Philipsburg. In the next war their great and peculiar achievement was at the battle of Fontenoy.

Louis in person had laid siege to Tournay: Marshal Saxe was the actual commander, and had under him 79,000 men. The Duke of Cumberland advanced at the head of 55,000 men, chiefly English and Dutch, to relieve the town. At the Duke's approach, Saxe and the King advanced a few miles from Tournay with 45,000 men, leaving 18,000 to continue the siege, and 6,000 to guard the Scheld. Saxe posted his army along a range of slopes thus: his centre was on the village of Fontenoy, his left stretched off through the wood of Barri, his right reached to the town of St. Antoine, close to the Scheld. He fortified his right and centre by the villages of Fontenoy and St. Antoine, and redoubts near them. His extreme left was also strengthened by a redoubt in the wood of Barri, but his left centre, between that wood and the village of Fontenoy, was not guarded by anything save slight lines. Cumberland had the Dutch, under Waldeck, on his left, and twice they attempted to carry St. Antoine, but were repelled with heavy loss. The same fate attended the English in the centre, who thrice forced their way to Fontenoy, but returned fewer and sadder men. Ingoldsby was then ordered to attack the wood of Barri with Cumberland's right. He did so, and broke into the wood, when the artillery of the redoubt suddenly opened on him, which, assisted by a constant fire from the French tirailleurs (light infantry), drove him back.

The Duke resolved to make one great and final effort. He selected his best regiments, veteran English corps, and formed them into a single column of 6,000 men. At its head were six cannon, and as many more on the flanks which did good service. Lord John Hay commanded this great mass.

Every thing being now ready, the column advanced slowly and evenly, as if on the parade ground. It mounted the slope of Saxe's position, and pressed on between the wood of Barri and the village of Fontenoy. In doing so, it was exposed to a cruel fire of artillery and sharp-shooters ; but it stood the storm, and got behind Fontenoy. The moment the object of the column was seen, the French troops were hurried in upon them. The cavalry charged ; but the English hardly paused to offer the raised bayonet, and then poured in a fatal fire. They disdained to rush at the picked infantry of France. On they went till within a short distance, and then threw in their balls with great precision, the officers actually laying their canes along the muskets, to make the men fire low. Mass after mass of infantry was broken, and on went the column, reduced, but still apparently invincible. Due Richelieu had four cannon hurried to the front, and he literally battered the head of the column, while the household cavalry surrounded them, and in repeated charges wore down their strength ; but these French were fearful sufferers. Louis was about to leave the field. In this juncture Saxe ordered up his last reserve—the Irish Brigade. It consisted that day of the regiments of Clare, Lally, Dillon, Berwick,

Roth, and Buckley, with Fitzjames's horse. O'Brien, Lord Clare, was in command. Aided by the French regiments of Normandy and Vaisseany, they were ordered to charge upon the flank of the English with fixed bayonets, without firing. Upon the approach of this splendid body of men, the English were halted on the slope of a hill, and up that slope the Brigade rushed rapidly and in fine order. "They were led to immediate action, and the stimulating cry of ' *Cuimh-niyidh ar Luimnrac agus ar fheile na Saesannach* '* was re-echoed from man to man. The fortune of the field was no longer doubtful, and victory the most decisive crowned the arms of France."

The English were weary with a long day's fighting, cut up by cannon, charge and musketry, and dispirited by the appearance of the Brigade, fresh, and consisting of young men in high spirits and discipline : still they gave their fire well and fatally ; but they were literally stunned by the shout and shatterred by the Irish charge. They broke before the Irish bayonets, and tumbled down the far side of the hill, disorganized, hopeless, and falling by hundreds. The Irish troops did not pursue them far : the French cavalry and light troops pressed on till the relics of the column were succoured by some English cavalry, and got within the batteries of their camp. The victory was bloody and complete. Louis is said to have ridden down to the Irish bivouac, and personally thanked them ; and George II., on hearing it, uttered that memorable imprecation on the Penal Code, " Cursed be the laws which deprive me of such subjects." The one English volley, and the short struggle on the crest

* ' Remember Limerick and Saxon faith.'

of the hill, cost the Irish dear. One-fourth of the officers, including Colonel Dillon, were killed, and one-third of the men.

Their history, after Fontenoy, may be easily given. In 1747, they carried the village of Laufeldt, after three attacks, in which another Colonel Dillon, 130 other officers, and 1,600 men were killed; and in 1751 they were at Maestricht. Lally's regiment served in India, and the other regiments in Germany, during the war from 1756 to 1762 ; and during the American war, they fought in the French West India Islands.

By this time they were greatly reduced, and at the Revolution completely broken up.

THE END.

J. M. O'Toole & Son, 6 & 7, Gt. Brunswick-street, Dublin